BREAK FREE

*Find Your Power,
Rewrite Your Story
And Create An
Awesome Life*

RONÈL M HARRIS

Copyright © Ronèl M Harris

1st edition, XII, MMXV

ALL RIGHTS RESERVED. No part of this book may be reproduced or transmitted in any form whatsoever, electronic, or mechanical, including photocopying, recording, or by any informational storage or retrieval system without the expressed written, dated and signed permission from the author.

Author: Ronèl M Harris
Title: BREAK FREE
ISBN:978-1-927892-45-9
Category: SELF-HELP/Personal Growth/Success

Publisher:
Black Card Books
Division of Gerry Robert Enterprises Inc.
Suite 214, 5-18 Ringwood Drive
Stouffville, Ontario
Canada, L4A 0N2
International Calling: 1 647 361 8577
www.blackcardbooks.com

....

LIMITS OF LIABILITY/DISCLAIMER OF WARRANTY: The author and publisher of this book have used their best efforts in preparing this material. The author and publisher make no representation or warranties with respect to the accuracy, applicability or completeness of the contents. They disclaim any warranties (expressed or implied), or merchantability for any particular purpose. The author and publisher shall in no event be held liable for any loss or other damages, including but not limited to special, incidental, consequential, or other damages. The information presented in this publication is compiled from sources believed to be accurate; however, the publisher assumes no responsibility for errors or omissions. The information in this publication is not intended to replace or substitute professional advice. The author and publisher specifically disclaim any liability, loss, or risk that is incurred as a consequence, directly or indirectly, of the use and application of any of the contents of this work.

Printed in South Africa

BREAK FREE

*Find Your Power,
Rewrite Your Story
And Create An
Awesome Life*

RONÈL M HARRIS

TABLE OF CONTENTS

PREFACE

A GLIMPSE OF RONÈL THROUGH THE EYES OF HER FAMILY

INTRODUCTION 1

PASSION AND DREAMS 3

CHAPTER 1: Beginnings Humble And Fearful 7

CHAPTER 2: Goodbye Hillbrow: Freedom At Last! 21

CHAPTER 3: School Girl, Housewife, Mother 37

CHAPTER 4: First Love 49

CHAPTER 5: "As God Is My Witness, I Will Never Go Hungry Again!" ... 61

CHAPTER 6: A New Life Again 73

CHAPTER 7: A Nasty Ghost From The Past 87

CHAPTER 8: Marriage And Motherhood 101

CHAPTER 9: Death Unforeseen 111

CHAPTER 10: Fate Took My Hand 123

CHAPTER 11: Back To Work 135

CHAPTER 12: Will It Ever Stop? 147

CHAPTER 13: Coming Home 161

CHAPTER 14: Montclare Revisited 173

CHAPTER 15: Forgiveness 181

CHAPTER 16: Diamond Years 189

CHAPTER 17: Full Circle 199

PREFACE

Dear Reader,

I wrote *BREAK FREE – Find Your Power, Rewrite Your Story And Create An Awesome Life* from my heart, with a sole purpose in mind: I want every woman to realise there is always a way to rise above any circumstances in life and that you have the power to change direction at any time. You are the writer of your own life story, you can decide how you want it to turn out – nobody else can write it for you.

I have chosen to share my life with you because I am a living (and thriving!) example of a woman whose past has no bearing on her present and future: No matter what has happened to you, there is always an escape route.

I am sure you will identify with some of my personal experiences, and I know you will find a set of guidelines and tools useful to assist you in making better choices to handle any difficulties life confronts you with.

This book has taken me more than a year to write because I've had to do my own healing while reliving some of the painful memories I intimately share with you. It has been a year of renewed self-discovery.

It has also been a year where my own tools were put to the test more than once!

In the past year, I have dealt with family issues, death in my inner circle and a personal health scare. At some point, it started feeling as if an invisible hand was interfering and trying to stop me from completing this book.

While writing the last few chapters, my beloved godmother, a special driving force in my life, sadly lost her fight with cancer. I will forever be grateful for the love she bestowed on me and I will always cherish her contribution to my development as a human being.

PREFACE

I would like to dedicate this book to her memory. Rest in peace, Aunty Rita . . .

The story of my life is told in chapters, chronologically ranging from my early childhood to the present. Every chapter is rounded off by my Anchor Pages, which were devised with you in mind. I included a summary of tools (suggestions) for your own use during embattled times, as well as to inspire you to start your new life as an empowered woman.

I welcome you on board this journey of self-discovery. Hopefully, my guidance will help you make better choices.

You can look forward to being the woman you are meant to be.

In friendship,

Ronèl Harris

A GLIMPSE OF RONÈL
THROUGH THE EYES OF HER FAMILY

"My mother's determination is evident in a favourite quote of hers: 'Never say never!' Three words she lives by. I see that as the essence of her positive outlook in life – her guts."

LEON MARINUS, eldest son

"My mother is a wonderful and caring person who is always happy. She also loves to make people around her happy. If my little sister or I am sad or unhappy about something, she will do anything in her power to save the day. I'm the happiest child in the world to have her as my mother. I love my mother very, very much."

JON-ROUX HARRIS, younger son

"What my mommy means to me: My mother is my idol. She is always there for my brothers and me. She always tells us to follow our dreams and to stay true to ourselves. She cares for us and helps us. She stays loyal to us and she always keeps her word. She is a wonderful mother and a fabulous wife to my daddy. But she is not just my mom – she is my best friend in the world. She always makes time for us when we need her. She is my smile when I laugh, and my shoulder to cry on. She motivates us and supports us. Her hugs make me feel safe and her smile makes me feel welcome. She is a strong person and she is committed to her work and always to her family. She tells us never to give up and to never stop trying. She is the best mom in the world. I know all the kids say that, but I know for a fact she is to us.

I love you, mommy.

From your baby girl, Danny"

DANIELLE HARRIS, daughter

"Ronèl is charismatic. She is a hard worker, an excellent mother and wife, and a caring human being.

My sister's nickname at school was Lucky; however, I believe I am the lucky one – after all, I found Ronèl.

Ronèl has blessed me with many things:

The gift of her love and companionship.
The gift of our two beautiful children.
The gift of conviction, to go for my dreams.
The gift of her fighting spirit.

She is my beautiful queen, romantic as an African sunset, yet with fierce green eyes and the will to survive like the animals she protects. She is a South African woman."

JOHN HARRIS, husband

INTRODUCTION

I am Ronèl Harris from Johannesburg, South Africa. I am a mother and I adore my kids. I am also a wife. I have been happily married to my husband John for 15 years. He is a very special man.

Then I am Ronèl Harris, businesswoman. A successful businesswoman.

I have wonderful friends and a family who is fiercely loyal and protective of me. I love German sports cars and I am blessed to enjoy spectacular African sunsets from my veranda.

My family and I share a beautiful home. We often escape to our farm in the bushveld and we are fortunate enough to spoil ourselves now and again with exotic holidays to faraway destinations.

It sounds like a fairy tale existence and sometimes, it does feels a bit unreal.

Why then, have I decided to write my story? Let me rephrase. *Why* do I want to share my *life* with you?

My life wasn't always this way and it is only because of the decisions I made, and by a more than generous portion of God's grace that I made it here. I believe that by sharing my story, I can help other women who may find themselves caught in the crosswinds of life, or who may be feeling overwhelmed by the seeming chaos of daily living by providing a fresh perspective.

I have endured abuse, I have suffered loss, I have known hardship and poverty, I have been broken, and there were times when I lost myself. But if you are honest about your 'lesser' qualities, it gives you the strength and courage to improve. It creates space in which to grow and to explore your psyche without fear of failure.

I know being honest about my insecurities makes it easier to work at strengthening my weaknesses every day. I know fighting feelings of self-doubt does not mean that you do not believe in yourself. It does not mean you have lost faith in yourself – to stop fighting would signify such a loss.

I will never forget the harsh lessons I learned in the cruellest ways possible, but I have always bounced back. And I will always bounce back.

I've had to start over from scratch three times in my life.

I firmly believe I am the creator of my own destiny – so are you.

We have the power to dream and turn our dreams into reality, and we have to be prepared to accept that we will never stop making mistakes. I see mistakes as gentle reminders that it is time for a much-needed reality check!

You have to believe you hold the key to a successful and content life in your hands. And you must believe nothing can stop you from achieving your dreams. The universe is generous; take the gifts that are offered to you. They are always special, trust me.

I am often told that I motivate people through my own zest for life. I started thinking about it, and yes, I embrace every second of life with passion and I seem to unwittingly take people along on my journey – you can also join me. The ticket is free of charge, but there are terms and conditions! No snags or catches, relax. If you want to travel with me, I only have one condition: You have to live every day to the fullest. That is not negotiable.

My whole life changed when I realised that I am the captain of *my* ship. It was *my* decision to become the captain of *my* ship on this journey through life.

My destination?

Life.

PASSION AND DREAMS

Remarkably, the following quote from an interview my eldest son gave to a journalist sums up the essence of my survival kit. Only two words: *Passion* and *dreams*.

"I always knew my mother was special and although we never really had much when I grew up, she always wanted to be better. My mother never gave into complacency. There were times when she did not know what to do or where to go. Times when she was down and out. But she always managed to survive through sheer *passion*. And nothing ever stopped her from *dreaming*."

Passion is a critical starting point towards realizing your dreams, which leads to your success in life. Your passion, your desire to become the person you want to be–the person you were meant to be. This is the real person but, sadly, some of us suppress it. Why then does it seem that women are especially prone to this phenomenon of suppressing their dreams? It could be due to many factors, including upbringing and conditioning, but moreover, I believe people's dreams stay as dreams because they don't actively pursue them. It is the same reason they don't win the lottery: They don't play . . .

I say: If you can dream it, you can own it. This is a very old quote and I know it is often dismissed as a cliché . . . If you are one of the cynical ones, you will find it difficult to have dreams and to make your dream a reality.

You are in charge of your dreams; you are the captain of your ship. Start visualising your dream, your new future. All captains can safely steer their ships to the most wonderful destinations if they adhere to the basics: Know where it is that you want to go, map out the best route to get there and use your compass to stay on course. Good captains will also pre-empt that there may be storms along the way; however, they are equipped with knowledge gained from experience, inner strength and wisdom to overcome that storm and put the ship back on course. But don't forget you have this equipment; you just need to choose to use your experiences to your advantage and not be anchored by it. However, if you don't lift your anchor to pursue your dream, you will remain a ship floating in the harbour forever. You will live and die without passion.

A dream lost.

You are the creator of your own destiny.

Although I had very little control over most of the obstacles in my life, I somehow never allowed myself to use this as an excuse to turn into a victim when I faced pain, sadness and failure later in life!

> *I believe people's dreams stay as dreams because they don't actively pursue them. It is the same reason they don't win the lottery: They don't play . . .*

In my adult life I still often find myself in one cul-de-sac or another on my journey. Road closures. Misleading directions. Wrong sign boards. These are not always circumstances beyond my control. I often read the map wrong and I get lost. I still make many mistakes. I slip often, but by falling, I get to know myself and learn new lessons from life's journey.

I learned the most important lessons the hard way. If you don't learn this lesson, the lesson will repeat itself until you learn from it.

I did not allow my mistakes and my failures to define me as a person. I was blessed to have the courage every time to get up, dust myself off, ignore the bruises and start over. Yet again . . .

I use every stumbling block as a stepping stone. There are many steps to success, but once you have taken the first step, every setback becomes a step closer to realising your dreams.

I have to admit, I was born with a head start, an advantage – and that is the innate strength of character and the fortitude to keep trying. I suppose some people will call it stubbornness, but I refuse to give up. I simply will not give up.

I have a good self-image. There were times, though, when it became a bit tarnished, but nothing a bit of spit and polish couldn't restore to its natural shine!

In spite of my inborn tenacity to survive, I had to work hard to develop my 'talent'.

And so I learned that we have choices . . . A simple choice. Every woman decides who she is and what she makes of her life.

She decides to follow her dreams.

> *"Leave your excuses and live your dreams."*
> – Paul F. Davis

"It's the unhappy people who most fear change."

– Mignon McLaughlin
(June 6, 1913 – December 20, 1983),
American journalist and author

CHAPTER 1

Beginnings Humble *And* Fearful

My mother fell pregnant with me when she was only 15 years old. During those years in South Africa, pregnancy out of wedlock was shameful and condemned by society. It left the 'unfortunate' girl with only two options. The first option was quietly disappearing to a home for unmarried mothers and, after giving birth, the baby was adopted and she never saw her child again. It was kept a secret. It never happened.

If a girl was lucky, her second option would be that the father of the baby would honour his 'duty' and marry her.

Whatever the girl's choice, (or rather her parents' will), she was not allowed to go back and finish school. The fact that my father was, according to the law of the country, guilty of statutory rape was quietly swept under the carpet and conveniently dismissed. He accepted his duty and married my mother. She accepted her fate and assumed the part of victim because of her circumstances.

My mother was an introvert, quiet and soft-spoken. I try not to remember how she looked later in life, but rather when she was still young and beautiful. She had beautiful long, dark hair, and when she went out to hang the washing on the line, I remember an auburn glow caught in the sun's reflections. I always remember her big brown eyes – like Bambi's. Innocent and slightly bewildered.

Forgive me if during the course of this book I come across as somewhat judgemental about my mother, which may seem a bit unfair. But if you continue reading, you will understand that the choices she made inadvertently moulded me into the human being I feel proud to see in the mirror every morning. I certainly would not have chosen her as a travelling partner on my life's journey, but I have to give her credit, albeit in a somewhat negative way. The image of the sorrowful woman, weak in despair, her life wasted, gave me strength. Watching her deteriorate every day, taught me the importance of dreaming and not accepting whatever cards life dealt me.

My father was a strong man who earned his living working in gold mines all over the province. Although I cannot remember much of my early years, I know we moved a lot. As a contract worker, my father needed to go where labour was needed. Whenever we moved, my mother dutifully packed and unpacked; she never complained or asked questions.

He was very good-looking, of the tall, dark and handsome type with piercing blue eyes and bushy brown hair. He possessed a deceptive charm, a forked tongue which he employed to get his own way; he had the gift of the gab. He was a master manipulator and my mother was his most adoring fan and victim. In her defence, she really loved him.

As a little girl, I dreaded Fridays. Miners were paid every Friday and my father would go out drinking with the boys. When he eventually came home, he was usually very drunk and my poor mother had to bear the brunt of his aggression. The moment I saw his car, I would gather my brothers and sisters and take them to the bedroom and make sure they were all quiet. Then I would go to the kitchen to be with my mother. I would sit on the floor looking down at nothing, waiting for the front door to open and close. He always closed the door by kicking one of his heels backwards. Then I followed the sound of his heavy miner's boots getting louder and louder as he walked closer into the kitchen. I stopped breathing. I never looked at him.

He never sat down normally. Instead of moving his chair back in the customary fashion, he kicked his chair out and into position before he sat down. I now think it was his way of digging in his heels, metaphorically speaking. Once seated, he kept quiet and soon the tension became unbearable.

After several minutes of deadly silence, he would start picking a fight. Like clockwork.

"What's this? Do you expect me to eat this garbage?"

His routine never changed when it was a 'Bad Friday'. Another plate was smashed to pieces. Sometimes, he swept it off the table on to the wooden floor; other times, it was flung against one of the cement walls or a kitchen cupboard.

Like an actress on stage repeats her words and actions, my mother would automatically start cleaning up the mess.

If she kept quiet, her silence was considered insolent and all hell broke loose. When she made an effort to comply by saying something feeble and harmless like, "Hello, did you have a nice day?" when he walked in, this would be his cue to go berserk!

It looked like he enjoyed beating his wife – it was his 'Friday Fun'. Sometimes, I found myself in the firing line, but he had to 'love' me afterwards so it was never more than a slap or two.

> *Forgive me if during the course of this book I come across as somewhat judgemental about my mother, which may seem a bit unfair.*

Every Friday, we sat frozen, waiting in the kitchen. We never knew what mood he would be in or what to expect. Or perhaps we knew exactly what the routine was. I waited for the sound of his big hand slapping her face. I tried not to open my eyes and I held my hands over my ears but I could never escape the explosive sound of flesh on flesh.

Sometimes he pummelled her with his fists. He didn't care whether they landed on her face or whatever part of her fragile body. The sadist revelled in his victim's suffering. He took pleasure in inflicting pain and relished in her pleading, begging.

My mother was not always blameless. Sometimes she started fights on a 'Bad Friday'; she sought to evade his wrath by reporting my 'disobedience', which was an instant trigger for his wrath. The first backhand was aimed at me, but then it was my mother's turn for spoiling his homecoming.

I struggled to understand why she never tried to get away from him. Why didn't she ever flee to one of the neighbours? Or phone the police? Or better still, leave him?

I suspect that she desperately wanted to believe him every time he apologised, the promises that "this was the last time . . ."

Famous last words . . . It never was the "last time." He was a good actor. Like Dr. Jekyll and Mr. Hyde, he could transform from a devil into the gentlest man, soft-spoken and apologetic at the drop of a hat. He would even beg for forgiveness holding a Bible in his hand, then read a few verses from it and pray.

Many years passed before I could shake my misgivings and trust God again, and attempt to read the Bible. How can a man indulge in drinking and swearing, viciously beat his wife, and the next day get on his knees preaching the gospel? At that age, I could not fathom or reconcile such extremes.

He did, at long last, fulfil his promise of the "last time" a few years later, but until that day, my mother tolerated his abuse. For almost 13 years, she never sought help and although I sometimes made an attempt to intervene, there was nothing I could do except to wait for the crying, screaming and swearing to stop, waiting for him to deliver the final punch or kick. I watched my mother crippled with pain as she staggered to their bedroom.

After she shut the bedroom door, she was out of the way. It would be my turn next. My heart beat so fast I could hardly breathe as I waited for my bedroom door to open. He always switched the passage-lights off, and I never saw him opening and closing the door. If I left my curtains open, I could see the dark outlines of his body coming closer. He habitually paused for a second or two before he made himself comfortable on my bed. Every time, he whispered a clumsy apology, something like: "I know I was not nice to mommy. I am so sorry, my baby."

> *I struggled to understand why she never tried to get away from him. Why didn't she ever flee to one of the neighbours? Or phone the police? Or better still, leave him?*

I closed my eyes but I couldn't block out the smell of stale cigarette smoke and cheap brandy; the sour smell of day-old sweat from working underground.

Then he 'loved' me. That's what he called it. "Love . . ."

I never responded. It felt like my tongue had dried up . . . I cried – without tears. As the years went by, I stopped being scared. My body did not feel part of me anymore; it did not belong to me. When he finished doing whatever he was doing, I would get a warning:

"You see what happened to your mother tonight? If you dare say anything to her, I promise you I will beat the hell out of both of you!"

Whenever I tell people the story of my life they always ask: "But how did it all start?" It did not just happen one day. I remember that when I was small, he always picked me up to sit on his lap. Like any loving father, I suppose. I would rest my head against his chest, feeling loved and protected. He stroked my hair. But then gradually, it all started changing.

I slowly came to realise something was not right. He started fondling me. Often even in the company of others, like it was the most normal thing to do! He touched me in a very clever way, hiding his hand from the rest of the company. Nobody ever noticed. The conversation continued casually while his hand gently caressed me between my legs.

"Come here, come sit on Daddy's lap."

It was a sentence I dreaded. If I hesitated, my mother would echo his request.

"Go and sit on Daddy's lap. Didn't you hear what he said?" From the tone in her voice, I could hear she was getting irritated.

> *That was only the beginning. The beginning of him showing me his 'love'.*

I suppose it is the most natural thing in the world, an adoring father with his young daughter sitting on his lap, but even though I was so young and didn't understand the severity of it all, I could sense that it was wrong. It made me feel like I was naughty. I knew I did not want him to do it. I did not say anything though, because one thing I did know was if he became angry, he wouldn't stop until somebody was bleeding.

That was only the beginning. The beginning of him showing me his 'love'.

It all changed one fateful morning when my mother put my baby sister in her stroller, took my little brother by the hand and announced, "Time for shopping and getting a bit of fresh air!"

I joined in the excitement of the moment, but not for long.

"Daddy does not want to stay here alone." My father looked at me, putting on his 'sad' face.

He was still drunk from the night before and had started drinking again early that morning.

"Yes, Ronèl, you stay here with Daddy. It would not be nice for Daddy to stay all alone. You can come with me another time. I'll bring you something sweet."

I just nodded and followed them into the passage, watching my mother wave us goodbye, then closing the front door behind her. "It is not fair! Why couldn't I go?" I wanted to cry but I knew tears irritated him.

I turned around. I got a fright. He was right behind me. "You stay with your Daddy because you love him? Hey? Daddy loves you too."

He picked me up and carried me to their bedroom. "You are Daddy's special girl. You know I love you, hey?"

He put me down on their double bed and started touching me. He then told me to touch him. I could sense this time he was different. Then, suddenly he was on top of me. He tried to pacify me, "Don't worry, it won't hurt."

He told me to be quiet and lay still. I remember looking at the ceiling when the most searing pain ripped through me! I will never forget the agony! I don't think I have ever been so scared in my life!

I started crying. I could not stop myself. I cried out in pain and begged him to stop!

"No daddy, no! You're hurting me!"

He used his big hand to cover my mouth. He didn't stop. Pain so much pain! It felt like my whole body was tearing apart!

Then all of a sudden, it looked like he realised what he was doing. A look of shock registered on his face when he saw the blood . . . he stopped.

> *"It is our little secret . . . Only between the two of us."*

I was going crazy, traumatized and in agony. The pain was excruciating, I couldn't move. I felt paralysed. He picked me up and carried me to the bathroom. I could not walk. He avoided looking at me; he just lifted me into the bath after he filled it and started washing me. He had to support me because I could not stand.

He apologised again and again, and kept saying, "I am sorry . . . I am sorry. Daddy loves you. Daddy will make it better, but shhh." He put his finger in front of his lips.

"It is our little secret . . . Only between the two of us." He gently touched my cheek, then he turned around and left the bathroom.

I watched in horror as the bathwater turned red.

Keeping Secrets

 ANCHOR

> *"Childhood should be carefree, playing in the sun; not living a nightmare in the darkness of the soul."*
> – Dave Pelzer, *A Child Called "It"*

When I started writing this book, I anticipated a response like, "Why should I read another story of a family's disgrace?"

But this book is not about a family's disgrace. Far from it. This book is about giving you the tools to learn to make better choices; it is about opening up different options to you and, most importantly, it will help you grow beyond the pain and hurt, and prevent you from ending up a broken, bitter person consumed with self-blame and self-hatred–even though you had no control over your circumstances.

When I eventually did try to alert my mother of what he was doing to me, she accused me of lying. "You're making it up, your father has his flaws, but I will never believe this from him! You are a little liar!" When my father arrived home later that same night, she told him what I had said–and he went berserk! That was one of the worst beatings I saw him give her: He dragged her until she was right in front of me and then cut her arm just above the elbow. The blood was dripping on the floor–he screamed at me. "See? Do you see what happens when you tell lies?"

I then tried confiding in my godmother. I thought she was the only person I could trust, but she also didn't believe me.

"Your imagination is running away with you. We all know your father is no angel but I can't believe he would go that far! You shouldn't spread rumours. You don't want your father to go to jail, do you?" From then on I kept silent.

> *I simply decided one day that it never happened. I convinced myself that it was all a figment of my imagination.*

So he continued to do whatever he wanted. I started fooling myself in a bid to banish images of him squirming on top of me. I buried all thoughts of his abuse. I pretended he never touched me, never hurt me . . . I never smelt him so close to me. I banned all memories of him screaming and swearing at me. I pretended he never did anything to make me feel worthless. I blocked everything relating to him, 'my father' from my conscious mind.

I simply decided one day that it never happened. I convinced myself that it was all a figment of my imagination. I took the easy way out, because nobody believed me anyway. I 'forgot' the horror of my father's actions. I erased every second, every instant, and every thought from my memory. So much so that it was only much later in life that I remembered how my father electrocuted a small kitten my godmother had given me. The horror of this act was simply too much to handle. He hated me loving my pet. In a fit of jealousy, he retaliated by being spiteful . . . no, evil.

 **COMPASS**

> *"Why isn't there a commandment to 'honor thy children' or at least one to 'not abuse thy children?' The notion that we must honor our parents causes many people to bury their real feelings and set aside their own needs in order to have a relationship with people they would otherwise not associate with. Parents, like anyone else, need to earn respect and honor, and honoring parents who are negative and abusive is not only impossible but extremely self-abusive. Perhaps, as with anything else, honoring our parents starts with honoring ourselves. For many adult children, honoring themselves means not having anything to do with one or both of their parents."*
>
> – Beverly Engel, *Divorcing a Parent*

Even though I was only five years old, I often wondered if other daddies also 'hugged' and 'loved' their little girls the way my daddy 'loved' me. I sensed something was wrong when he touched me 'there' in the company of other people. Even at that age, my instincts kicked in. For years I kept asking myself in despair, "WHY did nobody ever see?"

From then on, gradually over the next couple of years, his 'loving' changed from the beast that absconded with my innocence into one with an ever-growing appetite, stealing my childhood, and depriving me of a carefree and stable environment to which all children are entitled.

I resented my mother for keeping quiet and not seeking help, but I was also 'guilty' of keeping silent because he threatened to beat my mother if I dared say anything. I kept silent.

Until today, I believe she knew what happened when he came to my room at night or when he took me for a drive in his car. I believe she blamed me for the problems in their marriage as in her eyes, I became like any of my father's mistresses.

 VOYAGE

Children 'speak' without words, and as parents, or adults, we have to be present in their lives and in touch with their emotions and actions to 'hear' and 'listen' to these silent conversations.

Be present – listen without hearing. See – without watching.

If you are present and in touch with your child and his life, you will be able to notice the smallest behavioural changes. When I became hesitant to sit on my father's lap, my mother should not have forced me. She only needed to ask one simple question: "Why?"

If this chapter in my book can influence your way of thinking only in one way, I hope it would be the following:

Be present – listen without hearing. See – without watching.

Although abuse is prevalent in the household circle, mostly by a person trusted by the parents, it does not just happen in the home. Abuse can happen anywhere and by anyone, and because abused children often feel shame and/or guilt, they will keep quiet about it. The only way that you will know if your child is being sexually mistreated is to be present in his or her life.

If, however, you relate to this chapter because it refers to a similar childhood, I have to clear up all misconceptions you may have been carrying all your life:

You must immediately stop blaming yourself; you have nothing to feel guilty about! You did not do anything to deserve what happened to you.

Make a different choice today and change your life and your relationships forever. I have made it clear that I am not a trained professional, and my assistance stems from a shared experience and the most practical advice I can offer you is to stop suffering in silence. I am not naive to expect any person to change overnight, but you have to take the first step to recovery.

Find someone you trust, or preferably a skilled therapist, and find a way to talk about everything that happened. In my case, fate intervened, but I had to suffer a total breakdown to face my past.

"Sentiment without action is the ruin of the soul."

– Edward Abbey,
Desert Solitaire

CHAPTER 2

Goodbye Hillbrow:
Freedom At Last!

After living in a host of small towns, we ended up in South Africa's most infamous suburb, Hillbrow in Johannesburg, during the year I turned 12.

To some people it was a scary place, while others found the hustle and bustle exhilarating, but my memories of Hillbrow faded against our own immediate reality which remained consistent – no matter where we lived. A Friday was a Friday marked by fear. My father's drinking became worse and his violent behaviour increasingly more frightening.

For many years into my adulthood, I had nightmares of my mother screaming in pain, the same scenes playing over and over in my dreams. The smell of alcohol mingled with blood and the sound of breaking glass; my father shouting while he was beating my mother without any mercy. Seeing his silhouette in my door as he came into my room to 'love' me . . .

Back to our lives and times in Hillbrow. Although we lived in a small two-bedroom flat on the second floor in a building called Queen Anne, I never thought of us as being poor. My father squandered money during his drinking benders, but there was always food to eat and we were properly clothed. My mother did her weekly shopping and we always received presents at Christmas.

I remember one late afternoon when I helped my mother as she was getting dressed for a night out. Together, we took a lot of care applying her make-up and we tried a new hairstyle. She could hardly contain her excitement. My father had bought her a new red dress for this special evening out. I don't think I ever saw her looking more beautiful.

She was not the same beautiful picture when they came home later that night . . . I woke to the slamming of the front door, followed by his loud footsteps. I opened my bedroom door quietly and even through the small opening, I could clearly see my mother had been his punching bag again.

For many years I refused to wear anything red. It reminded me of blood and . . . that red dress.

One dark day, my father took his disgusting behaviour to a whole new level. I used to wash and polish the floors of one of our next-door neighbours every Saturday for a little pocket money, which I used to buy sweets for my little brothers and sisters. While doing my work, I heard a strange noise coming from the bedroom. I was convinced I was the only person in the flat so I went to investigate. I slowly opened the bedroom door only to be greeted with a horrific scene: My father in bed with the neighbour! He heard the door opening, turned around and saw me standing there. Laughingly, he ordered me to stand in the corner and keep my mouth shut. I wanted to run from the appalling display but I was rooted to the floor, indignant and traumatized.

"Stand there so you can watch and learn how to 'love' me back!" He looked at me with demonic eyes, while the woman continued to make moaning noises.

"You know what will happen if you run to your mother, don't you?" I nodded, fearful and revolted.

They seemed to enjoy the idea that someone was watching them! I closed my eyes. It was nauseating to think of my mother at home, totally oblivious about what he was doing while he was supposed to be at work!

I had to run! I knew I had to get away. I had no idea where I was running to, but I had to escape from the sickening experience.

I suddenly found myself outside the building and everything I saw reflected the gloominess of my mood. All the buildings looked grey and sad. A dash of colour caught my eye and I ran after it. It felt like I broke loose when I found myself in a small park filled with the most colourful blossoms which attracted my attention.

The mixture of bright colours immediately made me feel better – I imagined the flowers calling my name, which brought a smile to my face. The images I had seen in that smelly bedroom started fading . . . the beauty I was surrounded by calmed me down and made me feel a sense of God . . . in nature. I felt safe. Untouchable.

I started walking slowly around the park, feeling the leaves under my feet and smelling the scent of the flowers. I escaped into a whole new world. I made myself comfortable lying flat on the ground. At first, the light was a little bright and I had to close my eyes. When I could open them comfortably, I looked past the beautiful colours and the big blue sky opened up.

I started whispering to the heavens above, "Please don't let them find me, please don't let them see me . . ."

I don't know how long I stayed in the garden that day, but it became my sanctuary of escapism – whenever I felt down, my spirits were lifted by the colour of the flowers. I was always alone there, and I could safely retreat into a quiet space amidst the havoc of my life and the hustle and bustle of Hillbrow.

Meanwhile, Fridays came and Fridays went. Until one chilly Friday night in May. It was 1977. My mother and I were sitting at the table in the kitchen looking at each other in deathly silence, waiting for him to come home.

I remember thinking: "Please, please don't let him be . . ."

Before I could even finish my thought, my mother and I were both startled when he suddenly banged on the door.

"Open this door!" he shouted at the top of his voice.

"I said open the damn door before I kick it in!"

I jumped up from the table and ran to the door. "I am on my way, Daddy!" My brothers and sisters were already in their room.

My hands trembled while I tried to turn the key. He started kicking the door. My whole body was shaking.

"Hello, Daddy." I tried to sound normal but I could hardly get the words out.

"Where is that mother of yours?"

"In the kitchen, Daddy. She made Daddy's favourite food."

Shoving me out of his way, he stormed to the kitchen. He was drunker than I had ever seen him before. "Out of my way! Go to your bedroom!" I waited a few moments and then followed him into the kitchen.

"I said go to your bedroom, Ronèl!" He turned towards my mother, screaming at her. She was dishing up food for him. I could see her hands were shaking.

Never had I seen him so angry. He pulled his arm back making a fist, getting ready for a brutally hard punch, but he missed when my mother swiftly ducked away from him. He totally lost control and swept my mother's portable radio off the shelf. A blow to her head sent his plate of food crashing to the floor!

I don't remember much of the details of his attack that night other than the malice driving every punch and the obscenities he howled at my mother. All of a sudden, I realised she wasn't screaming anymore. She collapsed looking like a rag doll as she fell down to the floor. He carried on regardless, kicking her in the face.

She was lying on the linoleum floor, lifeless. My brothers and sisters came running to the kitchen, prompted by my frantic screams. Seeing my mother's body on the floor, they started crying uncontrollably.

I knew I had try and stop him, but I could not move. He was going to kill my mother if she wasn't dead already. I had to stop him! I stormed towards him and tried to pull him away from her. The kitchen reeked of a sickening blend of brandy, beer and the smell of my mother's blood. With my small fists, I attacked him from behind. "Daddy! Stop! You are going to kill Mommy!"

He turned around – a wild animal with dead eyes. He made growling sounds and punched me in the face with such force I fell against the kitchen door, the taste of blood filling my mouth. I quickly crawled toward the front door. I'm not sure how I managed to pull myself up, unlock the door and get out. I ran down the passage with him chasing after me. I was close to the staircase when he grabbed my dress, trying to pull me backwards. He lost his balance and pushed me down the flight of stairs. He was far too drunk to run after me. Every bone in my body felt broken. I was crying but nobody came out to help me. The excruciating pain was surpassed only by an overwhelming sense of loathing and anger.

> *I recognized the pieces of string to be the stitches the nurse spoke about . . . I counted seven.*

I ran to the closest call box not too far from our building. At first, the operator couldn't understand me because I was sobbing hysterically. I managed to calm down enough to explain that I wanted to make a collect call and to give her my godmother's number. When I finally heard Aunty Rita's voice, I could barely manage a few words. "Please help us! Mommy's hurt. She's lying on the floor. She's not moving!"

She told me to stay calm and she would call an ambulance, that everything was going to be okay. I ran back up to the flat to check on my brothers and sisters. When the ambulance arrived, I showed them to our flat. My father had locked himself in the bedroom and I assumed he had passed out. He couldn't give a damn what happened to her anyway. Before they lifted her onto a stretcher, I looked at her mangled face covered in bloody cuts. She was almost unrecognizable. I tried to speak to her, whispering comforting thoughts as they carried her down the stairs. My heart broke when they lifted her into the ambulance and shut the doors.

I cried while I watched the red light disappear down the street. I didn't know if she was going to be okay or if she was even still alive. I was terrified that I would never see my mother again, that we would be left alone with my father.

I turned around and slowly walked back to the flat. I closed the front door and locked it as quietly as I could. All the bedroom doors were closed. I went to check on my brothers and sisters again and I returned to the kitchen. I did not want the little ones to be confronted by the leftovers of the bloody mess my father had made. It was after 3 a.m. when I climbed into bed and, although I was exhausted, I could not sleep. I was haunted by the image of my mother's battered face, the gaping wounds, the dress she was wearing and her beautiful hair drenched in blood.

I couldn't help crying when, suddenly, I heard my door opening. I could not see him, but I smelled him. His smell coming closer and closer . . . slowly . . . to 'love' me. I closed my eyes, hoping he wouldn't stay too long, tears streaming down my face. Maybe if I had known that it would be last time he 'loved' me I probably would have endured it with a smile!

The next morning I woke up early and walked to the Hillbrow hospital. When I arrived at the information counter, I was taken to the emergency ward. I did not recognize my mother when the nurse pointed towards a bed. No, it could not be my mother lying there. They had cleaned her face and washed her hair, but her face was virtually covered with little black pieces of string – her eyes were so swollen she could not open them.

I touched my mother's hand softly. It was ice cold. With my other hand, I gently stroked her arm. I tried talking to her but she couldn't answer.

"She is hurting badly. Her injuries are severe," a nurse said to me while checking on my mother. "The doctor on duty really took a lot of care with the stitches – it shouldn't leave too much scarring and her ribs are also broken but they will heal." The nurse disappeared to check on another patient.

I recognized the pieces of string to be the stitches the nurse spoke about . . . I counted seven. The scars on her face remained for the rest of her life as a constant reminder of the day her husband almost beat her to death. The nurse couldn't have been more wrong.

Rocking back and forth in my chair, wincing as I touched my own bruised face, my whole body was sore and stiff, and I suddenly realised he could have killed us!

I turned to my mother. Without knowing if she could even hear me, I just started talking . . . rambling on and on about everything, the words just tumbling out of my mouth. "Look at me, Mommy! Why don't we just leave? How much more of this must we take? We cannot take much more! You know his apologies never mean anything. You must know what he does to me every time he comes to my room at night, when he comes to show me how much he 'loves' me. I know you believed me even though you called me a liar when I first told you. You saw the sheets covered in blood. You chose to believe him when he said he coughed it up, but you knew it was my blood, Mom, and not blood coming from my mouth either.

"When you came home after shopping and found me sitting in that chair . . . Please Mommy, you must stop pretending you don't know! You saw him carry me to my room that night because I couldn't walk! You know it wasn't because I was ill with fever!"

I became aware of the late afternoon light falling on us through the frosted-glass window. It was time to go home. I didn't want to leave my mother, but I was also worried about my brothers and sisters. I took her hand in mine and squeezed it tenderly.

Mother's Day is associated with fresh flowers. Though my mother woke in a hospital on this special Sunday, she took solace in knowing she was to be discharged. She was elated to be reunited with her children, but she couldn't hide the hurt and disappointment when my father wasn't there to meet her. He never went to visit her in hospital. I did not tell her that I had not seen him since he came to 'love' me after almost sending her to her grave.

To make matters worse, instead of Mother's Day cards and flowers, she received two ordinary pieces of paper. She recognized my father's handwriting on one and eagerly opened it first – it was the message she feared most during all the years of her married life.

"Sorry for everything I have done to you and the children. You will be better off without me. I will send you the divorce papers." This was her 'gift' from him on Mother's Day! The man she worshipped had left her.

I was ecstatic! He had simply walked out on his wife and five children and fled from his responsibility, like a coward leaving behind the broken remnants of his abuse.

It was almost too good to be true. I looked at my mother and, although her badly injured face disguised any expression, I could feel her anguish. Her eyes were too swollen to show the angst, but she needed no words to convey her sadness. She was shattered.

Something snapped in me when she started crying. It was difficult for me to understand – she should have been rejoicing!

Her hands were shaking when she opened the second letter. I could hardly hear her voice muttering as she was reading something about "eviction . . . unpaid rent . . . seven days . . ."

Her husband had not only rejected her, he had left her and us with nothing.

She wept distraughtly. I grabbed the letter from her and there it was, written in big red letters: EVICTION NOTICE.

My father's farewell present to his family was not only leaving us behind, but leaving us destitute and homeless. "Due to rent unpaid, you have seven days to evacuate the flat."

I was too young to understand these very serious consequences of his departure; that we had nowhere to go. The anger I felt at her a few moments earlier disappeared when I saw how heartbroken and worried my mother really was. Her husband had not only rejected her, he had left her and us with nothing. I took her hand and promised that I would help her take care of us.

"I will try to make sure that we always have food on the table and clothes to wear. I know it will not make any difference to the pain in your heart, but I will look after you and the little ones." I solemnly took this vow without having any idea what to do next or what it would mean. I knew only that I faced a new life without a father, with a needy, helpless mother and four siblings to care for.

Victims Of Circumstance

 ANCHOR

> *"All too often, abused women start to believe being 'punished' is a sign of commitment, an expression of love, and they learn to endure the beatings, the cruelty; they forgive and forget. When in fact, they know that the natural response to cruelty and abuse should be finding a way out into a safe place, out of harm's way."*
> – Ronèl M Harris

I used to wish that somehow my father's swearing and my mother's screams and crying would stop. The glass breaking, the nights I spent holding my brothers and sisters, trying to console them when they cried and begged me to help our mother. I tried, every time . . . I grew used to the coppery taste of blood in my mouth, but still I kept trying.

Physical and emotional abuse are treated as two different types of abuse, but I've put them in that order for a reason because I believe that if you are being physically abused, you are being abused emotionally as well.

My mother lived in a constant state of fear, trying her best to please her husband, knowing that no matter what she did or how hard she tried, it wouldn't be good enough and she would be punished.

I believe that the first time it happens you try to make sense of it all; you try to find a reason. You try to understand what you did to cause the outburst. If you know, you can try to prevent it in the future.

No matter how much you try, it will happen again and again. Eventually, you come to the conclusion that there is no point in reasoning. By the time you realise it is not about you, it will be too late.

It is very simple: You are (like in my mother's case) married to two husbands. One of them is gentle and caring (buying you a beautiful red dress), and the other person will leave you bleeding and crying on the floor. Emotional abuse should not be underestimated. It is just as dangerous as physical abuse. The perpetrator does not necessarily become physically violent, but breaking down the victim mentally – gradually – is as debilitating. There are no evident scars, and the perpetrators get away with emotional damage and psychological wounding.

My father was a master manipulator – a 'man's man', the soul of the party, everyone's friend, the entertainer, a loving husband and father in public. It would have been hard to convince people of the monster they knew.

COMPASS

I hope you never find yourself in a situation similar to my mother's, and my aim in this chapter is to make you aware of the signs and results of all types of abuse. I hope that I may, in some way, prevent it from happening to innocent women and children. If, however, I have raised alarms about your partner's actions, no matter how insignificant it may feel, you have to stop in your tracks and consider the following:

- Has he ever threatened to hurt you?
- Has he ever raised a fist as if he was going to hit you?
- Has he ever thrown an object at you?
- Has he ever restrained you?
- Has he ever pushed you around?
- Has he ever belittled you in front of others?

If the answer is yes to even one of these questions, you must accept that you are living with a potentially violent and abusive man. As difficult as it may be, you have to leave.

Believe me: One occurrence of violent behaviour is one too many. This man will not change, no matter how much you hope he will. And if you suffer in silence and you don't tell him his actions are unacceptable, hurtful and demeaning, you are only opening a door, inviting more violent behaviour in the future.

The first signs of emotional abuse are evident the moment he only as much threatens to hurt you. Trying to scare you with bully tactics as punishment for something you did and he does not 'approve' of is another early sign.

Have you ever had to worry (or even ponder) about your partner's mood when he comes home after work or a night out with the boys? Don't dismiss this as mere moodiness.

The man you are in a relationship with may be prone to violence if:

- He speaks disrespectfully about his former partners, blaming them for whatever went wrong in the relationship.
- He is disrespectful towards you or your friends, family or your children.
- He does 'favours' for you and boasts about his so-called generosity, which you should appreciate.
- He is controlling (wants to know your every move) and possessive (treats you like his property).
- He is never at fault – you or someone else are always to blame.
- He abuses drugs or alcohol.
- He pressures you for sex on demand.
- He gets serious too quickly about the relationship.
- He intimidates you when he's angry.
- He has double standards. He can go out with the boys, but has an issue with your friends.

As I said before, I am only guided by my own experience and with the exception of physical intimidation, please note that only one single characteristic mentioned above makes your partner an abusive man. Physical intimidation, however, is always a cause for alarm.

We have to be careful of creating stereotypes, because often – in South Africa – older, Afrikaans men from a previous era may exhibit a number of these behaviours because of the way they were raised, but they will also respect and protect their wives without ever abusing them or their children.

VOYAGE

> *"She was in a terrible marriage and she couldn't talk to anyone. He used to hit her, and in the beginning she told him that if it ever happened again, she would leave him. He swore that it wouldn't and she believed him. But it only got worse after that, like when his dinner was cold, or when she mentioned that she'd visited with one of the neighbors who was walking by with his dog. She just chatted with him, but that night, her husband threw her into a mirror."*
> – Nicholas Sparks, *Safe Haven*

Abusive men are not limited to a particular race or social background. Although it plays a part, upbringing does not always mould an abusive personality. Abuse is also not related to a man's IQ. There are no psychological tests to distinguish an abusive man from a peaceful 'normal' one.

An abuser tries to keep everybody – his partner, his friends and relatives – focused on how he acts so that they won't focus on how he thinks. I often think he believes that if you grasp the true nature of his problem, you will begin to escape his domination.

Abusive men are not limited to a particular race or social background.

What, then, should a woman do to protect herself from an abusive relationship?

When something doesn't feel right, you need to communicate clearly, and as soon as possible, which behaviours or attitudes are unacceptable to you and that you cannot be in a relationship with him if they continue.

If it happens again, stop seeing him for a substantial period of time. A warning that this time you "really mean it," WILL NOT WORK. You need to show him now that you mean it, that you will leave, that you will not tolerate the behaviour.

> SILENCE is an abuser's silent ally.

If he switches to other behaviours that are warning flags, chances are great that he has an abuse problem. If you give him too many chances even when the behaviour is different, you are likely to regret it later.

It is VERY IMPORTANT to be aware of the following:

SILENCE is an abuser's silent ally. If you feel that someone you know is possibly subjected to any form of abuse and you choose to remain silent (minding your own business) you become the abuser's partner in crime. This does not mean you must immediately go into attack mode and start making accusations. But be aware . . . be there. Listen to the answer when you call to find out why you haven't seen a friend for an extended period of time.

> *"To those who abuse: The sin is yours, the crime is yours, and the shame is yours. To those who protect the perpetrators: Blaming the victims only masks the evil within, making you as guilty as those who abuse. Stand up for the innocent or go down with the rest."*
>
> – Flora Jessop, *Church of Lies*

"It is not the strongest of the species that survives, nor the most intelligent. It is the one that is the most adaptable to change."

– Leon C. Megginson

CHAPTER 3

Schoolgirl, Housewife, Mother . . .

On a Monday, we all felt a bit lost in the big grey building in town where we had to see a lady from the welfare department. I did not understand much, but she took my mother through the procedures for us to become wards of the state. It meant my mother would be entitled to a state grant to assist her to take care of us. They would also provide her with a council house and make sure that we were all placed in schools.

All I understood was that they were giving us a house to live in! That's all I wanted to hear! I was ecstatic!

She drove us to an area called Montclare, with council houses built by the apartheid government to house unemployed, impoverished Afrikaners. Although they provided for us, I sometimes felt that they were hiding us . . . like a secret . . . something to be ashamed of, but I did not care. The houses were small and they all looked the same though painted in different colours. There were no carpets, just cold hard concrete floors – nevertheless I didn't care! We had a home, four walls and a roof to shield us from the elements – a safe haven.

> *All I understood was that they were giving us a house to live in! That's all I wanted to hear! I was ecstatic!*

Times were difficult. The council house did not come for free and my mother's grant was spent on paying the rent, coal for the stove, and what was left of that money was used to pay our account at Loonat & Son, the corner grocery where we could buy food on 'the book'. Every month, for one meal only, my mother would treat us and we would gorge on freshly baked rolls, viennas and coke. We ate like kings and queens! The cupboards were mostly empty, however we could always rely on my godmother. She never came to visit empty-handed and the local church sent us food parcels that helped a lot as well. Basically we were surviving from grant date to grant date.

The council houses were equipped with coal stoves on which to cook, but it was also a source of heat. During winter, it would warm up most of the house and we had the luxury of a hot bath every morning before school. My youngest brother was still a toddler when my father left us, and a baby needs warm water. We could only afford to buy one bag of coal every month, but when it was cold, it was not enough. So every morning, before daybreak, I left the house to collect the coal that dropped from the train wagons, falling onto the nearby railway tracks.

My mother was mostly withdrawn and disinterested; she still missed my father and her longing for him grew every day. I sympathised with her, I understood she was grieving. She was weak and while I tried to make her life as easy as possible, I gradually took on more and more of the responsibilities. I was willing to do anything just to keep her from looking for my father!

I could hardly believe it when, one morning, my mother was talking to me about the empty coal bin: "We are out of coal again . . . The coal truck will only deliver another bag next month and you know . . .

the children need to eat and bathe." She genuinely took no interest in anything, let alone her children. I thought she was finally getting over the loss of her husband! But no . . . that was just her hinting for me to make a plan to get more . . .

So the next morning, I woke earlier than usual. June has always been one of the coldest months during winter, but that morning was especially cold and grey. At 5 a.m. I was already walking next to the railway line. The air was thick with black soot coming from the chimneys of the identical council houses. The temperature was below freezing and my hands were burning before I started picking up coal. I remember the delight whenever I spotted another piece of coal – it was like finding treasure – but as time went by, every piece of coal became a curse, bringing with it stinging pain. My hands became frozen and without sensation, deadened. They turned blue due to the cold and my fingernails were still filthy from the previous day's 'scavenging'.

By the time I had gathered enough coal, the people in the houses were waking up. I was uneasy because I wasn't keeping up with my school work as I was always tired and hungry. That the children were growing fast and they needed more food and bigger clothes all the time also weighed heavily on my shoulders.

I knew I couldn't rely on my mother. Not only did she shrug off her parental responsibilities, she was never accountable if anything went wrong or for the circumstances we were living in. She was never at fault because she had no control over her life; she was the victim. Everything was always something, or someone else's, fault.

I had to do something to make money and after school, I went to see the owner at the grocery store a few blocks up on the main road. He told me that I was too young for them to employ me as a casual, but in the end I did manage to convince him to take me on as a packer in exchange for tips from customers instead of a casual wage.

I was willing to do anything just to keep her from looking for my father!

The church invited us to Sunday services. I was sceptical at first because the only religion I had known was my father waving the Bible around, forcing us to sing hymns when he was trying to atone for his violent outbursts on a weekend . . . I did not know God's grace, His love.

The more we went to church, the better I started feeling about our situation. My heart became lighter, the burden lifting, and seeing my mother sing along filled me with hope. We attended services for several months and my mother started meeting people, making friends and even socializing. It warmed my heart to hear her singing while she was keeping busy around the house or even in the garden. I truly thought that she had turned a corner in her life and that my dream of us living happily ever after was going to work.

I even started playing korfball, which became a definite highlight. We practised every Tuesday and Thursday, and I became the youngest player in our club to ever get provincial colours. Aunt Marge and Uncle Lappies helped me a lot. They assisted with getting me sponsorships for the relevant fees, as well as my gear.

> *"It's your father's fault that I am drinking! You will never understand it, but I drink because I'm so lonely without him!"*

On the court I felt like I belonged, like part of a team. It was an escape from my circumstances at home. My only escape. Even going to school was hard for me. I did not belong because the other girls did not like me. I was the outsider and I became a loner, most of the time spending breaks by myself sitting under a tree, not wanting to sit and watch the others eat their lunches. I rose above the hunger pangs by quietly dreaming of a better life.

Meanwhile, my mother was making friends in the area and socializing with the neighbours more regularly. At first I thought this was great, until she started drinking more and more and then every day. She started spending most of our money on alcohol. Then drinking brought about an even more alarming habit: She started enjoying the attention of male visitors with dubious reputations. I was dismayed by her behaviour especially because my brothers and sisters were now old enough to understand what she was doing. Shortly after this started, we stopped going to church services and, gradually, all the responsibilities for taking care of our home and my siblings fell on my shoulders.

Whenever I tried to talk to her about her wasting what little money we had, it would turn into a bitter argument, always ending with her in tears – the victim – and blameless.

"It's your father's fault that I am drinking! You will never understand it, but I drink because I'm so lonely without him!"

I worked harder, making sure the children were fed, bathed, did their homework, as well as kept our house clean, did my job after school, my own schoolwork and still picked up coal. It was slowly becoming too much for me to handle. One exceedingly cold night, after feeding the children what little food we had and putting them to bed, I dragged my tired body outside and from where I was sitting right under a lamppost. I could hear pieces of conversation while our neighbours were preparing to have dinner. The smell of food cooking, the sound of plates and cutlery exaggerated my own hunger pangs. I was miserable; I started crying. The tears running freely down my face had a salty taste. I was too tired and too hungry to worry about pride. I didn't care if the whole street heard me sobbing.

I heard someone call my name. I recognized the deep, gravelly voice to be that of our next door neighbour, Tannie Grieta.

"Ronèl, is everything okay?" I swallowed my tears and replied that everything was fine.

Tannie was never without a cigarette in her hand while sitting in her white cast-iron chair, drinking her favourite cola on her small stoep. She sat there watching the world go by.

"What's wrong, Ronellie? Come over here and tell me why you are crying, child."

I tried to explain that I hadn't made enough money again that day; that I only had enough to make sure the little ones have food. "I don't think I have eaten for two days!" I whimpered.

She looked at me for a moment, turned around and disappeared into her house. A few minutes later, she was back a plate overloaded with food. More tears followed, tears of joy though – I was completely overcome with emotion and gratitude at this kind gesture. I thanked her and promptly ran home where I called the children from their beds to join me for the feast! For once, we were just carefree children. We couldn't be bothered about anything, least of all table manners, as we laughed and teased each other! Genuine happiness filled our little house that night; we went to bed grateful and contented.

I took pride in our little home and even used the kitchen scissors to 'mow' the lawn. Many years later I was told that when people are fighting for basic survival, they don't worry about pretty, well-kept gardens. I didn't fit the profile. Being different earned me the nickname Sonskyn by the people in our street. I don't think it was always meant as a compliment though. It was possibly an implication that I appeared to be haughty.

I didn't think I was better than the rest of the people in our modest suburb, but then it wasn't altogether untrue – I was better in the sense that I had hope. I know I never looked like a girl living on welfare when I went shopping and later, when I started doing piece jobs. I always took care of my appearance. It wasn't that I was taller than other girls my age – it seemed that way because I walked tall. Upright. Proud.

The Price Of Freedom

ANCHOR

> *"Responsibility is the price of freedom."*
> – Elbert Hubbard

When we moved to Montclare I was a young girl of 12, but I was convinced that this was our family's escape from the prison called 'father'. I had visions of my mother and me running our little house together, working as a team to make a safe new home for us – I was so wrong.

I was far too young then to understand the concept and the extent of her dependence on my father. She moved from her parental home to the home she shared with her husband. I had no idea that this would mean that she would not know how to cope on her own.

If a relationship like this, where the woman is so reliant on her husband, comes to an end (by death or divorce), the woman is often left at a total loss. Like the wheel of a car suddenly coming loose and with the axle gone, it rolls away with no direction until it falls over.

 **COMPASS**

> *"If you want to be a slave in life, then continue going around asking others to do for you. They will oblige, but you will find the price is your choices, your freedom, your life itself. They will do for you, and as a result you will be in bondage to them forever, having given your identity away for a paltry price. Then, and only then, you will be a nobody, a slave, because you yourself and nobody else made it so."*
>
> – Terry Goodkind, *The Pillars of Creation*

One has to understand the nature of dependency: No matter how badly the person is being treated, or no matter how bad the situation is, there simply is no alternative.

There is, however, a way out: Be brave, take the first step and refuse to accept or encourage the same, bad behaviour.

You have to be completely honest with yourself, even if it is really hard. Take a look at the following and assess yourself:

- When your happiness is reliant on someone else – you are emotionally dependent on that person.
- When you are constantly seeking someone's approval – you are emotionally dependent on that person.

My father isolated my mother from her family. He did not encourage her to make friends, and he often bought the groceries and controlled the finances.

No matter how badly he treated her, she made a huge effort trying to please him, although she knew no effort would ever please him. It was almost pathetic to see her the day after a hard beating the night before: She was needy, passive and even clingy. Her biggest fear always was that he would leave her.

When your happiness is reliant on someone else – you are emotionally dependent on that person.

I unknowingly encouraged this dependent behaviour even further by stepping up and taking over the responsibilities after my father left.

 # VOYAGE

> *"I believe one owes it to oneself to make the changes to lead one away from dependency, rather than suffer the consequences of being too dependent on anyone for anything."*
> – Ronèl M Harris

You will need courage to overcome dependency and take back control over your own life – especially if you were not aware of your circumstances: That you were putting your life and your happiness into someone else's hands to control.

Nobody is entirely independent and even people who seem so strong are not as free as we may imagine.

The uneasy and difficult path to independence leads to peace, hope and happiness. The moment you admit to yourself you have a dependent personality, even only in that realization, you will start feeling calmer and happier knowing you are in control and you don't have to rely on anyone else for your happiness or financial support.

You need to ask yourself what you need emotionally. It can be a feeling of calmness, a feeling of safety, and a sense of purpose. Then you start in a small and simple way and gradually, you will become more confident to take charge of your life and achieve your dreams.

Make a note every time you do something for yourself and write down the feeling of satisfaction you get from it – this will encourage you to do it more often.

You may not have a dependent personality, but perhaps a friend or colleague does. The key to helping them is to refrain from doing things for them. You will help them by forcing them to do things themselves.

Nobody is entirely independent and even people who seem so strong are not as free as we may imagine. Our sense of independence often relies on what is happening in our lives at that moment – the trick is knowing that you can rely on yourself first and only seek help when you really need it.

Not because it's the easy way out.

*"You want
to believe that
there's one
relationship
in life that's
beyond betrayal.
A relationship
that's beyond
that kind
of hurt.
And there isn't."*

– Caleb Carr,
from The Salon Interview
(www.salon.com)

CHAPTER 4

First *Love*

One day, as I sat daydreaming during a school break, out of the blue, a boy approached me and asked if he may sit with me. Richard (not his real name) was three years older, boyishly handsome with messy blonde hair and piercing blue eyes. He lived in Montclare with his family as well, just one street below ours. He sat with me every break thereafter.

I enjoyed the attention and I was flattered when he invited me to meet his family. They were also dependent on a welfare grant, but they had a nicer home with better furniture because his brother worked somewhere and his father did odd jobs to earn a better living.

I would visit them whenever I had the time or when I needed to get away from the dismal atmosphere at our house. I was even invited to join them for dinner on occasion. I took great pleasure in being part of a family that spent time together. We would play cards and board games, and while I was with them, I could just have fun.

My mother did not approve of this so I had to sneak away to visit them. She never gave me a reason why, but I had the idea that she did not want me to have friends or to be happy.

The school regularly hosted 'sokkies' – school dances chaperoned by volunteer teachers and parents. Richard invited me along a few times, but my mother refused to let me go. It broadened the rift between us; the tenuous relationship we had was strained to a breaking point. It was as though she begrudged me the opportunity to be a carefree young girl; she preferred to have me bogged down in despair as she was.

Richard did not give up. Months later, he asked me again, and again my mother would not give her permission. "This time," I thought to myself, "she is not going to stop me!" I was very angry and determined.

> *I don't think I ever enjoyed an evening as much. I had such fun and I could not get enough of letting go of all my bottled up energy!*

As I woke on the day of the dance, a Friday, I immediately started planning: "How am I going to do this? How am I going to get out of the house without mother seeing me?" The questions kept twirling through my head. I didn't know if I would be able to go through with it! I doubted my decision because being devious was completely against my nature, but on the other hand, I was giddy with excitement and nervous energy; adrenaline was surging through my veins.

Going about my usual routine, cleaning and caring for my brothers and sisters, I washed my hair, ironed my beautiful polka dot halter neck dress with red trim at the seams (a treasured present from my godmother), and cleaned my shoes, being careful not to arouse my mother's suspicions.

As soon as my mother passed out from drinking, I dressed, brushed my hair and slipped out through the bedroom window, leaving it open just enough to open it again so that I could climb back later.

I did it! I snuck out of the house! While running to the school, I couldn't believe I actually had the nerve!

Arriving at the school hall, I was tense – it was my first sokkie and I didn't know what to expect. My daring escape, combined with the edginess, made me feel sick to my stomach. I was just about to turn and run back home when Richard was suddenly standing there, next to me. He smiled, took my hand, told me I looked beautiful, and we walked into the hall together. We definitely made an entrance because heads turned and people stopped talking, staring at us, at me . . .

We found a table and sat down, but not for long. He led me on to the dance floor and showed me what to do. I quickly picked up from watching the others too – I realised yet another new thing about myself . . . I had a natural talent for dancing.

I was mesmerised by the sparkling mirror ball and the twinkling lights, enthralled by the thumping rhythms from the turntable and I was hooked – I loved dancing! We sat down again to be spoilt with the vetkoek Richard bought us . . . they were scrumptious! We ate, drank our sodas and went right back to the dance floor – what fun!

I don't think I ever enjoyed an evening as much. I had such fun and I could not get enough of letting go of all my bottled up energy!

But like all good things, the wonderful evening had to come to an end. It was over too soon and Richard walked me home.

When we got close to our house, we whispered our goodbyes. My heart was still dancing; I felt like I was walking on air, but I came back to earth with a jolt! The window I left open to get back in was closed. My mother must have woken during the night and noticed I was not home – her decision to lock me out was born from spite, I'm sure. I had to spend the night in the outside toilet. It was freezing and in my haste to sneak out and get to the dance, I had taken nothing warm to wear. In the early hours of the morning, she found me curled up on the cold concrete floor, bundled into a corner with my arms wrapped tightly around me.

She started screaming at me, hitting me with a broom – the blows came down over my body and my arms as I was covering my head. She swore at me, exactly as my father had cursed her.

Instinctively, I jumped up from the floor, prompted by a sense of self-preservation. I grabbed the broom and pushed her away from me. "If you ever dare to do this to me again I will hit you back, this I promise you!" The last trace of my sympathy and respect towards her disappeared in that moment – we were at war.

We fought constantly but I would not buckle. I retreated to Richard's parents' house whenever I could, basking in the ever-present laughter and relaxed atmosphere.

One day, Richard asked me to go to the movies with him. I had never been to a cinema. I was thrilled at the prospect! We watched *The Champ*, starring Jon Voight. Not only was it the first movie I watched on the widescreen, but it was probably also the saddest. I cried so much I eventually had no tissues left! Like a true gentleman, Richard gave me his handkerchief. Then he kissed me on the lips. It was unexpected – he had never done it before and I froze. When we walked home after, he took my hand in his. I knew it was what all boys and girls did, so I allowed it. He kissed me again when we stopped in front of my house. I did not freeze up again, but it still made me uncomfortable. Sadly, I don't remember my first kiss fondly like most girls do.

> *The last trace of my sympathy and respect towards her disappeared in that moment – we were at war.*

A few weeks later, we were playing cards and listening to music as we have done on so many afternoons. We were laughing when Richard slowly inched his face forward and kissed me again. It was more intense than before, almost forceful. I started panicking. When he tried to touch my breast, I pushed his hand away . . . scared and confused.

"Sorry. I can't do this. I am going home."

He tried to apologise, but I was having none of it; I wasn't going to stay longer. Unwanted memories bombarded me. Memories I had worked very hard to forget! I avoided him for more than a week, but one afternoon after school, he stopped me on my way to the supermarket where I worked.

"I want to say that I'm sorry. I've missed you. Won't you come and visit us again? Please? I promise you I will behave. I will keep my hands to myself!" I could not look at him and it was a while before I could answer. "I will think about it, but you need to know I am not ready for that." He stayed true to his word. He behaved himself. In a little while, we lapsed into our comfortable and relaxed routine like nothing went amiss.

The children were growing up fast and I needed to work harder in order to make more money for food and clothing – my job packing groceries was not earning me enough.

Richard and his family never knew how dire my situation at home was, despite all the time I spent with them, but they surely suspected that something was wrong. I was weepy all the time and I cried at the drop of a hat. I wasn't coping anymore. I was feeling weary and worn out; I wasn't getting enough sleep. The children were growing up fast and I needed to work harder in order to make more money for food and clothing – my job packing groceries was not earning me enough.

I started dressing hair at the Old Age Home nearby for a small fee. I needed the money of course, but my actual reward was spending time with the old ladies. I loved listening to their stories of days gone by and hearing them cackling with laughter when they gossiped about something someone did. Most of all, I loved that I could make them feel good about themselves, hearing them coyly declare themselves and each other beautiful as they looked in the mirror when their hair was done . . . Their sincere appreciation warmed my heart to no end.

Daily life involved going to school, working two jobs and being a mother to my siblings. Every night, I came home to hungry little faces waiting for me to cook dinner. After they helped me wash the dishes and tidy up around the house, I had to help them with their homework, get them bathed and put them to bed. Only then could I start doing my own homework. My mother did nothing to help and I would sometimes wake up in the middle of the night still at the table where I fell asleep while doing my homework.

I felt exhausted, but I tried to keep up a brave face. I always managed a smile. I believed it was my duty to not make the children aware of any unnecessary problems or stress because they relied on me.

As if I did not have enough on my plate, I also found myself competing for Richard's attention. An older very beautiful girl at school had taken a fancy to him and she made no secret of her intentions. When I asked him about her and whether he was interested, he protested vehemently. I trusted him and believed him, but I worried nevertheless. We had been seeing each other for nearly a year and I was getting attached to him.

I decided to surprise Richard on my way home after work one afternoon. I walked into their house unannounced as I had done so so many times before, thinking I would just go straight to his room to find him listening to music or just dilly-dallying about as usual.

> *We had been seeing each other for nearly a year and I was getting attached to him.*

On this day, I was met by his mother and his brother in the lounge and before they could greet me, I whispered softly that they shouldn't let on I was there – I wanted to see the surprise on his face when I walked in. They looked at each other seemingly startled. Something was not quite right. They were acting strangely. As I turned around, they stopped me. His mother tried to whisper something, but I dismissed her hand on my shoulder. Knowing Richard would not be able to hear my footsteps on the concrete floor, I walked straight down the passage.

My heart was beating a mile a minute when I saw that his door was closed. Without knocking, I opened it. It made a squeaky noise. I was stunned – I couldn't believe my eyes! There he was, in bed with that girl – the same girl he professed not to be interested in. I don't know how long I stood there just staring. They were so caught up in the heat of their passion that they did not even notice I was in the room!

Tears started streaming down my cheeks; flashes of a smell from the flat in Hillbrow; images of my father two-timing my mother filled my head. Richard must have felt another presence in the room because he turned his head to look at the door. His face went pale. He didn't say anything. He looked me in the eyes and then turned back to her. Like I was not in the room!

My head was spinning and everything around me felt out of focus. I knew I had to get away, but my legs couldn't move. It took an immense effort to turn around and walk out of the room. I closed the door behind me. I did not slam it. Once outside, my strength returned and I started running. I could hear him running after me.

"Ronèl! Ronèl! Please wait! I want to explain! It's nothing!"

Nothing? How can he say it is nothing?

I did not look back, I ran faster. I just wanted to get away from him. For the first time ever, I just wanted to get home.

I cannot describe the humiliation, the hurt and rejection I suffered that afternoon, but after all these years, I still remember it like it happened yesterday.

> *For the first time ever, I just wanted to get home.*

My first love broke my heart. No, he ripped it apart! My life once again became mundane and dreary. I did not have an escape anymore; I had nothing to look forward to.

I was 15. We had been living in Montclare for three years. Three years of taking care of my siblings, working and studying around the clock. Three years of abject misery. Every day was an uphill battle. I hated my life, I hated my mother, I hated being poor.

I hated everything.

Broken Trust And Betrayal

 ANCHOR

> *"You cannot control what happens to you but you can control your attitude toward what happens to you, and in that, you will be mastering change rather than allowing it to master you."*
>
> – Brian Tracy

I was very vulnerable and fragile when Richard casually sauntered into my life.

I can't explain the devastation I felt when I walked into his room that day; the pain and rejection I had to face when I realised he lied to me.

> *I was hurt, humiliated and ultimately rejected because I felt I wasn't good enough.*

 ## COMPASS

In one afternoon, my life returned to the same dreary existence. Gone was Richard, my friend and my safety net.

> *Although BETRAYAL is a real part of life and it is unavoidable, your reaction and subsequent actions determine how successfully you cope with it.*

I was very angry that I allowed myself to trust him. I asked myself if this had happened because I would not let our relationship develop to a sexual level. I was hurt, humiliated and ultimately rejected because I felt I wasn't good enough.

- Can you remember your first love?
- Have you been betrayed by someone you trusted (family/friend/spouse)?
- If yes, did you blame yourself?

 ## VOYAGE

Betrayal is one of the most hurtful personal experiences in one's life.

When most of us hear the word betrayal, we immediately think affair.

Betrayal has many faces. Gossip behind your back, lies, a friend abandoning you, stealing from you or staging your downfall.

The essence remains the loss of trust. A friendship or relationship you thought was solid and grounded now lies shattered at your feet, and you are left to pick up the pieces.

Betrayal is complicated as it can leave you with difficult questions and choices, such as:

- What happened?
- What did I do to deserve this?
- Should I walk away and move on with my life?
- Is there a way I can pick up the pieces and save the relationship?
- What are my options?

You need to think clearly about whether you played a part in the betrayal or not. DO NOT automatically accept that it was your fault. Yes, you chose that person but no, you did not necessarily cause the behaviour.

REMEMBER

Although BETRAYAL is a real part of life and it is unavoidable, your reaction and subsequent actions determine how successfully you cope with it.

"There are three kinds of people: Those who make things happen, those who watch things happen and those who wonder what happened."

– Mary Kay Ash

CHAPTER 5

"As God Is My Witness, I Will Never Go Hungry Again!"

I was spiralling downwards at a breakneck speed. I could push no more, there was no fight left. I collapsed. I was in dire straits and I urgently needed help. A lifeline.

I found this lifeline in my godmother. As I mentioned before, she visited us once or twice a month. This visit was to be very different: She was greeted by the angst-ridden faces of my brother and sisters.

"We think there is something wrong with Ronèl, she doesn't look right," they told her in hushed tones.

She found me sitting on the floor in a corner in the kitchen, my arms hugging my legs close. "Ronèl? Ronèl, what's wrong, baby?" Putting the parcels on the table, she waved the other children away.

Years of bottled rage exploded when I heard the sympathetic tone in her voice. I couldn't stop myself. "No, Aunt Rita, no! I am sick and tired of picking up coal while it is still dark! I am tired of looking after the children! I am tired of cleaning everything and worrying about having no food to eat! I am doing everything to keep us going and my mother sits and drinks all day long! I am so tired! Tired . . . tired . . ."

> *"No, Aunt Rita, no! I am sick and tired of picking up coal while it is still dark! I am tired of looking after the children! I am tired of cleaning everything and worrying about having no food to eat!"*

I couldn't even cry or perhaps I knew that once I started crying, I wouldn't ever stop. I was not sure I had any tears left. I did feel a measure of relief because I had finally shared my woes – someone knew how wretched my existence was. Aunt Rita sat down on the floor next to me and put both her arms around me. "This has gone on far too long. You are coming to live with us. I am taking you away from all of this."

"I can't. What's going to happen to the children? I made a promise to them!"

"We will work something out. You need to think of yourself now. If you collapse completely, you won't be able to help them anyway." My godmother recognized that I had reached the end of my tether. "You've had to be an adult for too long now. I am taking you away. You will never get better here."

I don't know what would've happened to me if Aunt Rita didn't take me away. I don't want to consider it, honestly. Years later, I was told I had a total nervous breakdown. A nervous breakdown at the age of 15!

Living with my godparents opened an entirely new world to me. It was a world in which I needn't worry about where the next meal would come from; in fact, I had no concerns at all! It was liberating – I often felt at odds, yes, but I loved it.

Aunt Rita and Uncle Leon never had children so they made me their own. I only realised then how I much I had longed for this my entire life – a life without burden, a life I could live for myself.

I immediately felt safe but I had a long road of recovery ahead of me. I was emotional for quite a while still, but my godparents were very understanding. I felt physically weak and many nights I woke to my own screaming – I had terrible nightmares . . . nightmares that haunted me well into adulthood.

I felt terribly guilty about everything I now had. I felt that I failed them – I was going back on my word. By leaving my brothers and sisters behind, leaving them in my mother's care was effectively leaving them to their own devices. To me, that also meant they likely had no one seeing to their needs. Every time I ate, I thought of them and how they probably had to get by on empty stomachs.

While I had a beautiful room, my own room decorated in soft yellows, I had visions of my siblings having to make do with the bare minimum. When I snuggled into my warm bed at night covered in cosy blankets, I remembered the cold winters in my mother's house and I worried about them.

> *Living with my godparents opened an entirely new world to me. It was a world in which I needn't worry about where the next meal would come from.*

The biggest adjustment, however, was relinquishing control. Caring for my mother and my siblings, I became the captain of that ship for three years. Now, I had to suddenly live by other people's rules and sit back while they took care of me, but giving up my 'captaincy' was a small price to pay.

I watched a lot of television at first. It was quite a while before the novelty wore off; we never had a television set in our house. I especially liked curling up on the big green couch with a warm fluffy blanket when it was cold. I was safe and warm – I could barely believe my life now: No violence, no abuse, no hunger or physical labour. The sound of the fire crackling in the fireplace was very reassuring.

As I was flipping through the channels on the television one night, I came across an old classic, *Gone with the Wind*. I immediately identified with the heroine, Scarlett O'Hara. Fighting for survival in Montclare, I often fled into a dream world of make-believe. I took off on flights of fancy. I wanted to be like the beautiful and vibrant Scarlett. She was a free spirit and she loved life.

I was glued to the screen, held spellbound when Scarlett looked up at the sky, vowing to herself: "As God is my witness, I will never go hungry again!" I jumped up from the couch and imitated her. I pledged: "As God is my witness, I will never go hungry again!"

That film had an enormous influence on how I approached life thereafter. I decided to stop feeling sorry for myself. I swore that I would never stop dreaming. I would do whatever was necessary to reach my goals. It may sound naive and a touch mindboggling that watching a film could be a life-changing experience, but to me, fiction was fact – I had lived it!

The most powerful driving force was to keep my past alive and not bury it! I actively remembered the abuse in all its guises. I combined the pain, the hunger, the insecurities and the hatred, and I channelled it into an unyielding weapon – determination. It became my firewall. That was how I shouldered the hurt from my past and how I would protect myself from hurt and betrayal in the future. I went back to school, even played sports and made friends. I could act my age.

"As God is my witness, I will never go hungry again!"

Soon, the only reminder of my dreadful childhood was the niggling disquiet regarding my siblings. My godparents still took me to Montclare every Tuesday and Thursday evenings to practice korfball, after which we would pay a short visit at home, but that was as close as I got to my old life.

I had been living with my aunt and uncle for almost a year when a friend at school introduced me to her brother, Shaun (again not his real name). She boasted of how handsome he was and she was not exaggerating – he was gorgeous! We started dating and my godmother adored him. I couldn't shake the memory of Richard's betrayal though, so I could not allow myself to fall in love, but I did enjoy spending time with him and I did enjoy the attention.

> *Faithful to the vow I made alongside Scarlett O'Hara, I knew I could only help others if I was strong within myself.*

There were still times when I was a slave to self-pity. I still had moments of self-indulgence, asking why these horrible things happened to me! Why did some people live blissful lives, while others, like me, suffered endlessly? Why did a select few know nothing but joy, and yet others know only sadness?

As if I conjured it, a little voice inside would answer, telling me that there was a reason I survived so much pain and distress . . . I was special, I had to be – obviously I was strong enough to overcome whatever curveball life may throw at me. I proved as much.

I slowly came to recognise that I was infused with vigour, an intrinsic sense of self, of preservation, and the courage to do what had to be done. There was no longer any foundation for pessimism. The lifeline my godparents extended to me changed everything. They patiently guided me towards healing, helping me to trust again.

When I was settled and I felt more confident, my aunt arranged a part-time job for me. After school, I worked at the bank where she worked. I was almost 16 and I knew that I would soon have to brave the adult world. I had two years left before I would have to earn my own living. I needed to save money for college and send money home.

Receiving my very first decent paycheck was unforgettable! I could afford to go shopping and I did. I bought a new dress and a stunning pair of new shoes. I still love shoes, but I don't think I appreciated any pair of shoes thereafter as much as I did that first pair bought with my first salary.

I could finally support my brothers and sisters too. Every week, I sent money home religiously, but I took care of myself first. Faithful to the vow I made alongside Scarlett O'Hara, I knew I could only help others if I was strong within myself.

I enrolled at a college and I proudly paid for my studies. My achievement would be solely mine – I was the captain of my ship! After completing my college course, I was ready to start knocking on the doors of the world and to knock loudly! I was invited to my first interview for a permanent position. I was gushing with anticipation. Not for one second did I have any idea that walking through that door would change the course of my life dramatically.

Forever.

Fortune Favours The Brave

 ANCHOR

> *"You must give everything to make your life as beautiful as the dreams that dance in your imagination."*
> – Roman Payne

Many new experiences were waiting to welcome me when I moved in with my godparents. Not only was it a life without burdens, it was a life I could live forever. A life where I felt loved and cared for. A life which invited dreams!

I could dream!

I have always been a dreamer – but now my dreams turned into technicolour! My new circumstances and the introduction of television opened a whole new world to me.

The profound impact of Scarlett's words still live on in me today: "As God is my witness, I will never go hungry again!" I repeated her words, I made an oath, and I have never failed that promise to myself.

> *I have always been a dreamer – but now my dreams turned into technicolour!*

One of the big changes in my life was Friday nights. My godfather slowly started changing the terrible connotation of 'bad Friday nights'. He introduced playing cards on a Friday and it became a ritual.

For the first time I also made new friends at school. I felt I fit in with my clean school uniform and my own lunchbox. I had the courage to sit with the other children; I was not an outsider anymore and even though I was the new kid, I settled in quickly. I was just another girl and I loved every moment of it.

I also tried to keep my promise of looking after my siblings when I started working part-time after school. Keeping promises is a very important part of who I am.

> I cannot stress the importance of having dreams enough. Turning your dreams into reality is the ultimate achievement.

My dreams grew bigger and I became more inspired – even adamant – to make a success of my life. I would work hard and learn as much as I could not to follow in my mother's footsteps. I made a decision to have a beautiful life to compensate for the hardships and difficult times.

Even then I knew it was up to me to make my dreams come true and I could not rely on anyone else. I was going to work hard. For me.

 # COMPASS

> *"Hold fast to dreams*
> *For if dreams die*
> *Life is a broken-winged bird*
> *That cannot fly."*
>
> – Langston Hughes, *The Collected Poems of Langston Hughes*

I cannot stress the importance of having dreams enough. Turning your dreams into reality is the ultimate achievement.

Despite seldomly getting support from others, I never allowed any negative discouragement to slow me down. I continued to work for a better tomorrow and I still pursue my dreams today.

You can ask yourself the following questions:

- Have you been told that your dreams are a waste of time?
- Did you just give up on your dreams because life was just too complicated or hard?
- How actively are you pursuing or working on your dreams?

> *I believe the only obstacle to living our dreams are the lies we keep telling ourselves by making excuses.*

 **VOYAGE**

> "You may have been born on the rubbish dump. But be careful not to believe that the rubbish dump was born in you! Your environment may try to set conditions that may attempt their fingers on crippling you. But you've got to stand and say, 'I thank you Lord that I am rising against and above my limitations.'"
>
> – Israelmore Ayivor

It doesn't matter where you come from – it is only important where you are going.

You can't let your past steal your dreams from you because of your own insecurities or what people say. The best way to sidestep this is to pursue all your dreams – actively.

You only have one chance at the life you've been given and if you don't put your dreams into action, they will remain dreams.

- Do you remember what your dreams were?
- What are you doing to achieve them?
- Do you have a plan?
- What is holding you back from achieving your dreams?

I believe the only obstacle to living our dreams are the lies we keep telling ourselves by making excuses. Stop making excuses and ignore the opinions of others. Don't let anything or anyone stand in your way.

- Stop procrastinating today.
- Write down your dreams and a plan of achieving them.
- Actively work towards your dreams every day.
- Keep your promises – start with the ones you make to yourself.

Write down your dreams and a plan of achieving them.

"Do one thing every day that scares you."

– Mary Schmich,
"Advice, Like Youth,
Probably Just Wasted on the Young"
(*Chicago Tribune*, 1997)

CHAPTER 6

A *New* Life Again

I arrived for the first interview of my new working life and although I did not know it then, I had arrived at a momentous turn which would change the course of my entire life.

As I walked through the door, dressed to impress of course, I noticed how very handsome the man behind the desk was. When he stood up from his chair I couldn't miss his tall frame, being a tall girl myself!

"Hi, I am Leon Rossouw. You must be Ronèl?" He stretched out his hand to introduce himself.

> *I dutifully kept sending half of my salary to my mother to buy food for my brother and sisters.*

"I am pleased to meet you!"

I couldn't get a word out. I knew I had to pull myself together and stop acting like a schoolgirl. While he conducted the interview, I noticed his soft brown eyes, which lit up every time he smiled.

> *She was just sitting there, apathetic and quite obviously drunk, holding a cigarette in one hand and a glass of brandy in the other.*

I was awarded the job as a receptionist and I worked very hard. Happy to have a foot in the door to prove myself, I made it my business to learn about all the different departments, their functions and what every position in the company entailed. Within 18 months, I was promoted and became the youngest salesperson on a senior level. I wasn't about to stop there. My aim was set on the next level: Sales Manager.

Absorbed as I was in building a career and securing my future, I was still very aware of my family's plight – after all, I dutifully kept sending half of my salary to my mother to buy food for my brother and sisters. When memories of my struggles faded, I was reminded of their desperation. One day, I received a call from my brother saying there was no food in the house.

"How is that possible? I sent her money yesterday."

"I know, but she went to the bottle store!"

I left the office and walked to the train station. I was fuming when I stepped onto the first train headed to Montclare. The closer I got to the Newlands station, the angrier I became. I sincerely resented my mother. Why didn't she go out to work? I knew without question that she had no regard for herself, but how could she so completely disregard the well-being of her children?

Disembarking the train, my fury had taken on a life of its own – it was beyond control. When I opened the door, I couldn't believe the sight in front of me. There was nothing left of the beautiful woman I remembered. She had lost so much weight because of her drinking and not eating properly. She was just sitting there, apathetic and quite obviously drunk, holding a cigarette in one hand and a glass of brandy in the other. I don't think she even realised I was standing in front of her.

> *He gently lifted my chin so as to look into my eyes as he told me softly, almost whispering, "I am falling in love with you."*

I exploded.

Slapping the brandy glass out of her hand I started screaming at her, but the louder I yelled, trying to break through the fog of indifference, the less she seemed to care. My mother could not give a damn! I felt so infuriatingly helpless and, before I could stop myself, I slapped her. When I realised what I had done, I turned around and fled. I realised I was enabling her destructive habit so I stopped sending her money and started taking groceries and food instead every Friday afternoon.

That altercation, and the shock of seeing what my mother had become prompted me to work even harder – I would never be like her. In a short time, I was promoted to the position of the youngest ever Junior Sales Manager.

The atmosphere in the store where I worked was quiet and restful. Customers spoke in soft tones, I could hear furniture being moved and, further away, traffic in the street. I was also keenly aware of the store manager shuffling papers in his office. I could hear the noise of his chair when he stood up from his desk, and as he came closer to my desk, I smelt the familiar odour of his cologne.

I realised I was smitten with Leon Rossouw. He was 12 years my senior and I had the biggest crush on him. It was the first time I had felt anything like that and it was further complicated because I was riddled with guilt – Shaun and I were still dating. He was in the army and at that stage he was posted in Rwanda. We wrote endless letters to each other. I sent him parcels and we phoned each other every Friday. When Shaun came home on a weekend pass, I introduced them to each other.

"He likes you," Shaun told me. I laughed and brushed off his words, but secretly I hoped he was right! I was taken aback by how blasé I was being about it, but I guess being in love can make you do strange things. I kept questioning myself, trying to fathom why this was happening. It was a dead-end anyway, I thought, because a man like him would never be interested in a girl like me. Nevertheless, I could not deny what I felt. I was not familiar with the sensation, thus I did not know what to do about the butterflies fluttering in my stomach every time I heard his voice or saw him! I was head over heels in love, and I loved the feeling!

One evening, we worked late doing stock take. Everyone had already left and I was getting ready to go home when, suddenly, Leon stood in front of me, unnervingly close. My heart skipped a beat but I tried to act casually, avoiding his eyes.

He gently lifted my chin so as to look into my eyes as he told me softly, almost whispering, "I am falling in love with you."

Unbelievable! The man I had been quietly dreaming about for months shared my feelings. I just stood there, looking at him. Suddenly, those were the most beautiful words I had ever heard and they were spoken to me!

"I know you are involved with Shaun and I will respect that. I will wait."

I did not say anything but my heart was thumping wildly in my chest! "Can it be true . . . is this for real?" I asked myself over and over.

I opened my heart to Leon and told him that I felt the same, but because I was still in a relationship, we decided to keep it under wraps. We started having lunches together, but he was adamant about me continuing to write to Shaun. But my letters became stinted, more and more matter-of-fact – mostly just reporting routine happenings.

Our romance was slowly developing, but the looming presence of my boyfriend cast an unmistakable shadow. Shaun's military service had come to an end and while organizing his welcome home party, I battled my guilt. I knew that time was running out – I was going to have to tell him, I was going to break his heart.

I felt that I had to tell my godmother who had already started planning my wedding to Shaun before the party. She had already made her mind up that she wanted him to be her son-in-law and she told me that almost daily, saying that once his service was over and he was home, we could start planning the wedding. I, on the other hand, thought only of ending it with Shaun so that I could be with Leon. The thought of us being able to openly express our devotion, to freely love each other, overruled my consternation about breaking up with Shaun.

> "How can you treat me like a child? I am a working woman!" I felt humiliated.

I did not look forward to bursting my godmother's bubble, but somehow I thought she must've seen the signs that I was in love, that it wouldn't come as too much of a surprise. I was convinced that everyone must have noticed the change in my behaviour. I was walking around with my head in the clouds. I couldn't wait to get to work every morning just to see him, to know that he was somewhere in the building.

I couldn't have been more wrong. My godmother was absolutely livid when I told her I was going to break up with Shaun because I was in love with Leon. It was the first time she was ever angry with me. An ugly argument followed and I understood that she was not going to make it easy for me.

Leon arrived at our house on his motorbike one Sunday morning. He had invited me to go on a breakfast run with him. I couldn't wait for him to arrive and when I heard the sound of his motorbike coming up the driveway, I ran to open the front door but my godmother beat me to it.

He climbed off his bike and walked up the driveway towards us. I thought he looked dangerously sexy in his leather outfit. He politely introduced himself to her before greeting me. My godmother ignored his courtesy and without any hesitation, I heard her saying, "Sorry for making you come all the way, but Ronèl is not coming with you!" She closed the door in his face. When I heard him starting his bike again, I burst out in tears. My godmother and I had the most horrible fight ever, screaming at each other.

"How can you treat me like a child? I am a working woman!" I felt humiliated.

"As long as you live under my roof, you will not see that man! He is too old for you and you know that! Your mother was seduced by an older man and she paid dearly for it!"

I could not believe she was comparing Leon to my father! How dare she! However, she continued: "Why do you think he is divorced? Do you want to deal with the baggage of his daughter with another woman? Stop your nonsense! Shaun is the right man for you!" Enraged, I stormed to my room and cried myself to sleep.

An unwelcome surprise was waiting for me when I arrived home from work the next day. My godmother had invited Shaun to our house. How could she do that? Especially after I told her in no uncertain terms I was in love with Leon! How could she simply ignore my feelings?

My relationship with my aunt became heavily strained. I never thought it was possible because I loved her so much. She had given me a new lease on life and I felt beholden to her, but now she tried to discount my feelings for the man I loved. She aggressively tried to keep Leon and myself apart. We did not stop fighting and said awful things to each other. I was not going to give in to her demands and spend my life with a man I didn't love.

> *"I want to thank you for everything you have done for me. I will never forget your kindness and I will always love you, but you forced me choose. I am sorry."*

I tried many times to tell her how much I loved him, how wonderful a person he was, that I wanted to spend my life with Leon, but she absolutely refused to get to know him. Every time I suggested that they ought to meet properly, it resulted in a fight. Leon and I had been dating for three months, but I could still not invite him home.

Leon did not take it personally and he told me to be patient, that she would come around to the idea of us eventually. The next time he invited me I told my godmother that I was going on a breakfast run with him whether she likes it or not: "You are not going to stop me this time! And you better start accepting it because I am going to marry him!"

She replied calmly, carefully stressing every word: "If that is the case, Ronèl, I think you better leave my house." I was stunned. Her ultimatum saddened me, filled me with fear – I had nowhere to go, but I was not going to stop seeing Leon.

The next day, I enquired about accommodation at a hotel not far from my work. It was not the nicest of places and it was also not the cheapest, but it meant we could see each other without the interference of my godparents.

I went home, packed my clothes and a few belongings. "I want to thank you for everything you have done for me. I will never forget your kindness and I will always love you, but you forced me choose. I am sorry." I left. We stopped talking altogether. I missed them, but I knew it was the right thing to do.

A month later Leon took me out and when I saw the restaurant, I knew it was going to be a special evening. A band was playing lovely music and in the flicker of the candlelight, he looked more handsome than ever. Holding my hand, he looked into my eyes like he did when he admitted he was falling in love with me.

> *My ship was leaving the harbour when I was only 17. I was appointed in a (my first) permanent position, and I had no idea my life was about to change drastically in a short space of time.*

"You are everything I have ever wanted in a woman. You make me feel alive and I want to spend the rest of my life with you." His words sounded like they came from a storybook, but I knew they were genuine. He was the star of a movie – the hero – and I was the woman he loved– his heroine. But it was not a movie.

He went down on one knee and the band had stopped playing. Everyone in the restaurant was looking at us. He opened a small box, took out a ring and asked me to be his wife. I could hardly breathe and I just sat there, staring at him. I felt like everyone in the restaurant was waiting for my reply.

I eventually managed to say, "Yes! Of course I want to be your wife!"

He picked me up and while holding me tightly to him, he turned me around and around. Everybody started cheering and the band started playing again! I was in seventh heaven! I felt like a princess!

Changing Tides

 **ANCHOR**

> *"The captain of a ship can run a great ship, but he can't do anything about the tides."*
> – Ronèl M Harris

We have to know that the tides in our lives change without any warning. The seas will be calm and your ship will be sailing smoothly when, suddenly, a crosscurrent pulls you off course – either temporarily or permanently. That is up to you.

 **COMPASS**

Allow me to illustrate:

My ship was leaving the harbour when I was only 17. I was appointed in a (my first) permanent position, and I had no idea my life was about to change drastically in a short space of time.

The first tidal change came from the home front. I was working hard settling in and learning as much as I could. Then I received a call from my brother saying that they didn't have food. I had to make the trip there to see what was happening to the money I sent home every week. A very ugly confrontation with my mother followed when I saw the state she was in.

> *Would you agree we can sometimes be stuck, and the tide needs to change before we can move on?*

During this time, I realised that I was falling in love with Leon even though I was still in a relationship with Shaun – a test for my morals and values. In the end, it was Leon who showed me that by doing the right thing (continuing to write and send parcels) and waiting for Shaun to return from the border before ending the relationship, I would be able to move on without feelings of guilt.

My ocean suddenly became very rough, the tides pulling and pushing in all directions.

The change in tide following my decision to leave Shaun that nearly knocked me over was Aunty Rita's reaction. She would not accept Leon, and I had to leave their home and move into a hotel. Harsh words were exchanged during an angry confrontation. It broke my heart.

My work was very fulfilling though, and of course I enjoyed spending time with Leon. I worked hard and getting a promotion rewarded me. Leon asked me to be his wife, and it felt like my ocean was once again settling down. I started looking forward to the voyage.

- Can you think of a specific time when your tide changed suddenly?
- Do you remember the cause and effect? What were the consequences?
- How did you react when your ship's course changed suddenly?
- If another sudden tide change had to happen in your life right now, would your ship sink?
- What, if anything, would you do differently, armed with more knowledge?
- Would you agree we can sometimes be stuck, and the tide needs to change before we can move on?

 # VOYAGE

Being able to deal with our daily lives and the changing tides that come along takes a substantial amount of self-control. You need to be able to keep a tight grip on your steering wheel, have the tenacity to move with the tides, and be strong enough to brace yourself against the waves trying to throw you off course.

People often forecast doom when life is good by warning, "It's a period of calm before the storm!" Living your life from such a viewpoint is not necessarily pessimistic, unless you find yourself constantly living in fear of it.

Being prepared that life will not always be smooth sailing is a very healthy approach. When the tide does suddenly change, it allows you to be calm and have a clear perspective.

The key is to understand that you don't live in isolation. People and circumstances have the power to cause tide changes. How you deal with these changes and the consequences (your adaptability to change) will determine if your ship sinks or if you manage to weather the storm.

> *There should be no doubt, no nagging "what ifs" or "maybes". I have a rule that I always remind myself of: If in doubt, don't do it.*

COULD HAVE, SHOULD HAVE. BUT, WHAT IF . . .? THEN IN THE END . . . DIDN'T . . .

The decisions we make in our lives are often the cause of tides changing – this is why it is important to carefully weigh your options against the possible outcomes.

Deciding what you want and whether the consequences will be acceptable are decisions only you can make. There should be no doubt, no nagging "what ifs" or "maybes". I have a rule that I always remind myself of: If in doubt, don't do it.

As a young teenager, I made a promise to take care of my siblings. But working in another town, I sent money to my mother every week, entrusting her to take care of the children.

The winds, the sea, and the moving tides are part of our natural surroundings. It is up to you to discover the wonder and beauty and majesty they may hide.

When I realised I could not rely on my mother and could not trust her with the money, I decided to send groceries instead. When the children needed anything, I took it to them. Consequently, the conflict between us became worse, because my mother now only had the money that was left over after the rent was deducted, to squander on alcohol and cigarettes. We became even more estranged and eventually stopped having any contact altogether.

A consequence of the confrontation with my mother was that it led to a big tidal change in her life, and she was forced to find temporary work for four months! She started looking after herself and started socializing in a healthier way, even playing korfball twice a week. Although we were still on bad terms, I felt proud of her for trying. This consequence of my tidal change was definitely one I could live with!

Falling in love with Leon was a beautiful surprise, but the choice to be with him was one of purpose. I could never have foreseen the effects of this decision: It never crossed my mind that Aunt Rita would react the way she did.

I could easily have decided to put an end to the conflict by giving in to Aunt Rita's demands to stop seeing Leon and instead to marry Shaun. I chose my happiness instead and accepted the consequences of my decision, which meant having no contact with my godparents. I held firm to my belief that this could be resolved once they saw how happy we were together.

I am sure you can relate in one way or another to the effects of changing tides in your own life. Decisions made, paths chosen, and the cause and effect it had in your life.

REMEMBER THIS . . .

The winds, the sea, and the moving tides are part of our natural surroundings. It is up to you to discover the wonder and beauty and majesty they may hide.

The fact that there are analogies in my book about the sea is not without deliberate thinking and planning, because no one could write truthfully about change without mentioning the tides of the sea.

"Courage isn't the strength to go on — it is going on when you don't have the strength."

– Napoléon Bonaparte

CHAPTER 7

A Nasty Ghost *From The Past*

It was a week after our engagement and the entire affair with Leon was surreal – I had to pinch myself to check that I wasn't dreaming. I still couldn't believe it was really happening to me. I was in love with a man who treated me like a princess and I was excelling at work. Life could not be better!

Driving to work one morning, I stopped at a traffic light not far from our store. I was fantasizing about my future, merrily humming a love song while waiting for the light to turn green. Absently scanning the sidewalk, I went ice cold. For a bleak moment I thought I recognized my father standing there, about to cross the street. I turned my head away, quickly and very deliberately – it couldn't be him, it was years since he abandoned us. I would likely not even know him if I ever saw him. Convinced that I was imagining it, I turned my head back and looked straight into my father's eyes! There he was, like a nasty ghost from my past.

I was unravelling, coming apart. "No it can't be! Why is the light not going green?"

I thought that if I just denied the grim fact, I could unmake it . . . if I did not believe it couldn't be true. But I knew I had not mistaken the recognition in his eyes. He had seen me. The blood drained from my body and my throat closed up in fear – it felt as though I could not breathe. On the brink of hysteria, my foot hovering over the accelerator, I rebelled against providence. An indignant rage took a hold of me! I contemplated running him over. Why, after all these years? Why now? What sick twist of fate brought me to this? I could not think straight. I wanted to kill him before he destroyed my hard-won happiness.

> *I turned my head back and looked straight into my father's eyes! There he was, like a nasty ghost from my past.*

Something inside me snapped and I just knew I had to rid myself of him for good. I turned the steering wheel and pressed down on the accelerator – the car jumped and swerved towards him but he saw me coming and he jumped out of the way. I just missed him. We both knew exactly what I had attempted to do. I dissolved in a frenzy of tears.

It took a massive effort to pull myself together before I walked into our offices a few minutes later, but I could not hide how upset I was. Leon immediately sensed that there was something wrong with me. I hardly noticed anyone as I walked straight to my desk and sat down. There were no friendly greetings and no smiling as I did every other morning. Within seconds Leon was there, wanting to know what was wrong. I just looked at him, tears streaming down my face. I couldn't say anything.

He knew nothing of my past before I came to live with my godparents. I could not imagine sharing the sordid details of what my father had done to me. I had relegated all those horrors to my past but here he was, back from nowhere, back to torment me. As if in a scene from my worst nightmares, there he was, standing right there in the same street where I worked, in the same part of the city. I could not believe it was happening to me.

Leon asked me to come to his office. He was worried about the state I was in.

"I saw my father on the way here. I haven't seen him in years!"

"Is it such a bad thing? I mean, he is your father."

I interrupted him, almost screaming, "Yes! Yes! He is . . . a bad thing!"

I tried to concentrate on my work, but my father's face kept appearing in front of me. I was filled with a debilitating fear. Fear that he would come for me. I went home early. I needed to be by myself. I would have to explain my reaction to Leon and I needed to figure out how I would tell him.

> *His appearance had reduced me to precisely that: A frightened little girl.*

I strove to persuade myself that he could not harm me anymore; I was no longer a frightened little girl – I was a grown woman. He wouldn't dare touch me again. But the mere thought of him being this close filled me with fear – his appearance had reduced me to precisely that: A frightened little girl.

On my way back to the hotel, I was exceedingly wary. It felt like my father was everywhere, skulking in alleyways, hiding behind pillars. I had to make sure he wasn't following me. Even behind a locked door, I did not feel safe. I could not sleep that night.

I was still anxious when I arrived at work the next morning. I was tired and drained. I sat at my desk, but it was a fruitless exercise; I couldn't focus no matter how hard I tried. Around 11 a.m. I sensed a presence, someone looking at me, and I just knew this time it was not paranoia. He was standing right in front of my desk. I looked up; I looked straight into his eyes . . . eyes which I prayed I would never see again.

I went utterly numb.

In a voice that sounded strange to my ears, I managed to ask, "What are you doing here? What do you want?" I wanted to run, but I remained calm. I was not going to let him intimidate me. I was about to stand up from my desk when I felt Leon's reassuring hand on my shoulder.

"Good morning. I am Peter, Ronèl's father. Pleased to meet you," he said, offering his outstretched hand. In my ears, his voice sounded like he was talking down a drain pipe, echoing.

I felt like I was looking at the scene that followed from the outside in. I heard Leon inviting him to his office for coffee. It felt unreal, dreamlike, like I was having a nightmare and I couldn't wake up! But it was really happening. I could not believe the man's arrogance. He had simply come to my office; he had the audacity to walk back into my life as if nothing ever happened. Moreover, what about me? What was wrong with me? Why didn't I just chase him away or better yet, call the police?

I was caught in limbo, trapped between a nightmare and a living hell. I could not move. I don't know how long I just sat there staring into space. Then with a jolt, I remembered he was with Leon and suddenly, I was moving, running to his office. I came to a dead stop when I saw him shaking Leon's hand. My father turned to me, smiling. "Leon has just told me the two of you are engaged. Congratulations, I am happy for you, my daughter!"

I wanted to run, but I remained calm. I was not going to let him intimidate me.

I lost all reserve when he came towards me – I started screaming, "Don't you dare to touch me! Stay away from me!" I don't remember anything after that. I fainted. When I came to, I saw Leon's worried face leaning over me, gently wiping my face with a wet cloth. Then it all came crashing back! It was him! My father was back and in this very office! I started looking around but I could not see him anywhere. No, it was only the two of us . . . Had I imagined all of it?

Only when Leon said, "He left," did I realise I wasn't losing my mind, it had really happened, he was really here. "I'm taking you home now; I will get your car back to you later."

I was mortified. He was forcing his way back into my life. There was no way I could avoid it anymore – what was Leon going to think when he finds out how my father corrupted me? Will he think me used and filthy? Will he leave me and if he didn't, would he ever look at me like he used to? What was I supposed to do? How do I tell the man I love I was raped by my father? Rape, the mere word made me shudder – traumatized anew. I have never considered it like that, but that is exactly what it was! I had been raped repeatedly by my own father!

When Leon brought my car later that afternoon, I was waiting for him. All afternoon, I rehearsed how I would reveal my disgrace, mentally preparing myself that he would leave me once he knew. When he walked through the door, I just blurted it out. Without looking at him, I told him everything that my father had done to me. I never wanted to tell him about this; I never wanted him to know, but I had no choice.

"I am so ashamed, I will understand if you want to leave me. I don't blame you."

I was too scared to look at him. I could not bear seeing the disappointment on his face, the disgust or even hatred I had prepared myself for. "I am so ashamed, I will understand if you want to leave me. I don't blame you." I had no tears left. I closed my eyes and pointed at the door, "You don't have to come back."

But instead of walking out of my life, he put his arms around me. He was crying as he assured me of his unconditional, undying love. "I will never let him hurt you again. Never!" he promised.

> *I despised the fact that the man I hated more than anything in this world would be at my wedding; that it would be him sharing in these precious, unforgettable moments with me.*

I fell asleep in his arms, feeling absolutely safe for the first time in years. When I woke up the next morning, he was still there. Purposely, he repeated his words of the night before: "I will never stop loving you. I am with you forever and I will not allow him to ever hurt you again! Let's get married – it is long overdue!"

I did not think it possible, but I loved him even more.

I was, however, not yet 21 and, as such, a minor. The law stipulates that a minor has to have parental consent or that of a legal guardian's, in order to get married.

It had been months since last we spoke but I phoned my godmother. Putting my pride in my pocket, I told her that Leon and I were to be married and asked, "Will you please be my witness? I really want you to share this moment with me." She knew I needed her consent. She simply hung up. I could not ask my mother either; we had no relationship to speak of. I was not her daughter; I had been further reduced to a source of income, but since I stopped sending money, I was no longer even that.

I felt rejected and a touch lonely, but nothing would detract from my joy. I was the happiest girl in the world! I spent every lunch break looking for a new dress. We were getting married in court, but I wanted to look stunning nonetheless. I didn't care about a fairy-tale wedding; I just wanted to be Mrs. Rossouw – that was my happily ever after.

Back at the office after lunch one afternoon, I was still lost in a daydream when I saw Leon making angry gestures while talking to someone sitting opposite him. I could not see who it was. I asked a colleague about it. She whispered: "Your father is with him. They have been talking for almost an hour now."

I felt instantly sick and I ran to the bathroom. My head was spinning, a jumble of questions whirling in my mind. I'm not sure how long I hid in the locked cubicle but eventually, Leon knocked on the door. "Open up! We are going to apply for our marriage license!"

"But how? You know I don't have anyone to sign on my behalf!"

I followed him into his office. "Your father is willing to sign." I was dumbstruck. "Your father alleges he is a changed man. He admitted everything he had done to you to me; he wanted me to forgive him. He assures me that he is very sorry for the pain and suffering he caused you. He begs you to forgive him. He wants you to give him another chance."

"Never!" I felt like screaming it from the rooftops. "I will never forgive him!"

True to form, he was saying all the right things, anything to serve his purpose. He was only ever interested in his own well-being. He was superficial and selfish and quite obviously just trying to soothe his own conscience. I quietly asked, "Can he give me back my life? My childhood? My innocence?" I stood up from my chair. "Never! He can rot in hell – I hate him!" I walked out looked at my father and said: "I hate you!"

Leon understood the pain I was feeling; he came to comfort me. "Relax now. I told him that wasn't happening, you suffered too much. I also told him to stay out of our lives. If he really meant what he said, that he was sorry, he had to sign you off."

Negotiating with my father was hard for Leon – he wanted to kill him, but we needed his signature in order to get married. He made him promise to leave us in peace thereafter. Forever.

I despised the fact that the man I hated more than anything in this world would be at my wedding; that it would be him sharing in these precious, unforgettable moments with me. I was not going to allow him to spoil my day, however, so I simply ignored him. In my mind, he was not there. When the officer of the court finally declared us husband and wife, my father tried to congratulate us, but Leon stopped him short. "Leave now. Don't say anything, just leave. We have an agreement."

Emboldened and elated by my new status as Mrs. Rossouw, I said: "Yes, leave and forever stay out of my life. I will never forgive you!" He looked at me with the same sad puppy-face he used to manipulate me when I was a child, and then he walked away.

Impervious to anything but him, I flung my arms around my darling husband's neck. He was my hero, my everything! He tenderly kissed me and I was ready to spend the rest of my life with him.

When Your Past Won't Stay Buried...

> *"The past is never where you think you left it."*
> – Katherine Anne Porter, *Ship of Fools*

I was walking around in cloud nine. I could only think of my beloved Leon, our happiness and how in love we were. My past never crossed my mind anymore, and the only reminder of my old life was when I delivered groceries to the house in Montclare.

 ANCHOR

> *"Your past is always your past. Even if you forget it, it remembers you."*
> – Sarah Dessen, *What Happened to Goodbye*

Fate intervened one sunny morning. My past decided to remember me. It was like my father appeared out of thin air. It was like watching a tornado approaching, then continuing to destroy everything in its path and there is nothing you can do. Only watch.

My entire life, each and every memory from my past came flooding back – moments I buried far from my conscious mind. Surprise turned into rage when the reality of his presence sunk in. "How dare he have the audacity to just . . . appear again?"

Fate intervened one sunny morning. My past decided to remember me.

Because I had not seen him in so many years I thought I'd never have to deal with him again, and because I stored the memories so far away, I did not even think of sharing my past with Leon. My first thought was, "If he knows, what will he think of me?"

I immediately predicted the worst-case scenario: "He's going to leave me."

The saying, "You can run, but you can't hide", took on a very real meaning for me when my father walked into my office and stopped right in front of my desk!

 # COMPASS

> *"We are products of our past,*
> *but we don't have to be prisoners of it."*
> – Rick Warren, *The Purpose Driven Life*

I made a huge mistake to think that I could bury my past and all the memories that came with it. I know now I reacted like that because I refused to deal with everything in my childhood.

I was harbouring feelings of shame and guilt, and I simply could not cope with the enormity of it all.

- Are you burdened with feelings of guilt or shame about something that happened in your past?
- After my mother and Aunt Rita dismissed me, saying I was making up stories, I never confided in anyone about being raped by my father. Has something happened to you that you feel you can't speak to anyone about?
- Are you blaming yourself for something that happened to you in your past that you had no control over?

You need to take your head out of the sand and face up to every bad and sad thing that has happened to you. This is the only way to set yourself free and continue to live a fulfilled life.

You can't keep on looking over shoulder, afraid of your past catching up with you, because it will. Just like my past surprised me in an unguarded moment. Had I been better prepared, I would have dealt with the situation much better without any of the devastation it caused.

Everybody has a past. Whatever happened to you in your life is part of your journey – it brought you to your where you are today. It is part of your here and now.

- Is your life on hold due to unresolved issues in your past without you realizing it?
- Are you battling with relationships because of trust issues?

> *Are you burdened with feelings of guilt or shame about something that happened in your past?*

The night, I told Leon everything about my past. I was ready to say goodbye to him. I was convinced he would walk out of my life, never to return.

To my surprise, he stayed and the bond between us became intensely stronger. I knew then, more than ever, that he truly loved me when he took me in his arms and cried with me.

- Are you afraid to let people get too close to you out of fear they will find out about your past?

What Are Your Fears?

 **VOYAGE**

Have you ever been told to . . .

- "Just let go."
- "Just accept it."
- "Just get over it."

And your immediate response was, "That's easy for you to say, when you have no idea what I've been through!"

Do you realise that they are right, and the only reason they don't have an idea what you've been through is because you never told them?

> *Introspection shows you what is lacking or needed in your life, which immediately gives you clarity and direction.*

The benefits of facing your past are valuable beyond measure.

If you understand that you are in control, you will have peace.

Introspection shows you what is lacking or needed in your life, which immediately gives you clarity and direction.

You will gain power through your action instead of feeling disempowered due to your previous inaction.

Most importantly, you will gain freedom from the chains of the past that bind you.

> *"It's being here now that's important. There's no past and there's no future. Time is a very misleading thing. All there is ever is the now. We can gain experience from the past, but we can't relive it; and we can hope for the future, but we don't know if there is one."*
> – George Harrison

"It is not until you become a mother that your judgment slowly turns to compassion and understanding."

– Erma Bombeck,
*Motherhood:
The Second Oldest Profession*

CHAPTER 8

Marriage *And* Motherhood

Marriage never featured in my hopes of a better life, but saying "yes" to the man of my dreams was the easiest decision I ever made! I knew it was the right thing to do. He gave purpose to my life. He taught me what real love was and how to love without fear. My husband treated me with reverence, like gold, and I became a member of a well-adjusted family. My new life was filled with laughter, happiness and love, but there was one snag.

Being a married couple meant we could no longer work together in the same store; company policy. Luckily, I was offered a position as head of department at another nearby store. Of course, I took the job. Not only was I fulfilled on a personal level, my career was flourishing as well.

> *Saying "yes" to the man of my dreams was the easiest decision I ever made! I knew it was the right thing to do. He gave purpose to my life.*

Soon after we were married, Leon decided to start his own business. We didn't have much to begin with, but we had an abiding love, a passionate romance and a dedicated friendship. I was living my dream and living it alongside someone I trusted implicitly.

Shortly after we were married, I fell pregnant. I was jubilant. Caring for my family trumped having a career. I wanted to be a full-time mother because I was afraid that I might fail – after all I did not have the best example. I did not want to end up being like my mother. I was nervous, but when I gave birth to a beautiful healthy baby boy, I was bursting with pride and ready to accept the challenge of motherhood.

We were husband and wife foremost, but also best friends and parents to a beautiful baby boy. We were soul mates.

My happiness knew no bounds and when my dear godmother arrived on our doorstep, with a beautiful Maltese puppy as a peace offering, my delight was complete. "All that matters is your happiness," she said and admitted it was plain to see that Leon was a wonderful person. It didn't take long before they were firm friends!

Life couldn't be better despite the fact that the pawnshop Leon invested in was not a success. He trusted the wrong people and we lost everything. Sadly, it was a big blow to his confidence and his self-esteem suffered. He wanted to provide for me more than anything; he wanted me to feel secure. He desperately wanted me to have the best in life!

One morning, there was a knock at the door. It was the Sheriff of the Court and his colleagues. They walked in and listed everything we owned. Leon was declared bankrupt. They took everything – they left us with a few kitchen utensils, our double bed and the fridge. The fridge was a concession because I was pregnant.

Yes, I was pregnant again and we couldn't have been happier. We lost everything but our love never faltered. We moved to a small little house on the outskirts of town and we improvised with our few possessions. I did not mind our circumstances. I still felt safe with him, coveted.

Every day was special. He left little notes for me to find in unexpected places like the fridge, or when I lifted a cushion while cleaning the couch, I often found a special message, a declaration of love.

Leon soon had another job but he did not earn much. For a while, we ate porridge three times a day, but at dinner he would light candles, making me feel so special. Life was beautiful.

He worked very hard while I turned our humble cottage into a home. Slowly but surely, we were picking up and rebuilding our lives together again. We planned our future; we made a great team. We were husband and wife foremost, but also best friends and parents to a beautiful baby boy. We were soul mates. I was happier than ever before. I was deeply in love with my husband and I loved being a mother.

Soon, Leon's hard work paid off. He was promoted at work and the excitement was electric – it rippled throughout our little house. On the day it was to be made official, Leon seemed reluctant to leave the house. He would walk to the door but then double back.

I felt perky throughout the whole day, full of life. Almost dizzy with happiness. It was a day for merriment. They were planning a party at the office and I was invited, but I came down with 'milk-fever'. I called to tell him that we would celebrate together at home.

Naturally, he was going to be late because of the office party. Delicious smells wafted through our cottage. I cooked a special dinner and our baby was bathed and fed, blissfully asleep. Around 7 p.m., I was ready. I styled my hair for the occasion and put on my new red dress (yes, RED – it may have been symbolic for how far I had come in my emotional healing – Leon and the safety of his love), I was waiting for my handsome prince to come home . . . It would be soon!

I kept looking at my watch. It was past 8 p.m. – he was much later than anticipated. I called his office and Leon sheepishly apologised, "Sorry, Baby, but the boys insisted on one for the road! We will leave in a few minutes. I'll be home soon," he told me in that voice I loved so much.

Two hours later, I had a premonition of Leon having an accident but I shrugged it off. I thought my mind was merely playing tricks on me but as time passed and it became later and later, I became increasingly agitated. I went to our room to feed our son and I must have fallen asleep with him cradled in my arms.

The Adventure Of Motherhood

 ANCHOR

> *"Your children are the greatest gift God will give to you, and their souls the heaviest responsibility He will place in your hands. Take time with them, teach them to have faith in God. Be a person in whom they can have faith. When you are old, nothing else you've done will have mattered as much."*
>
> – Lisa Wingate, *The Prayer Box*

When baby Leon was born, I was so scared I didn't know what to do, even though I helped raise my siblings. Having my own little baby was totally different. I can only laugh now about my nervous clumsiness during that time.

Because I grew up in a dysfunctional family, my expectations of being a mother, motherhood and the role of a mother were of the utmost importance to me. My baby had to feel safe and loved. That was the most important thing to me. I stopped working so I could spend every minute with him, and even though we struggled financially, it was worth the price we paid. We made it work, because Leon and I worked as a team to make ends meet.

 **COMPASS**

> *"Parents can only give good advice or put them on the right paths, but the final forming of a person's character lies in their own hands."*
> – Anne Frank, *The Diary of a Young Girl*

I see each new achievement as a sign from God that I'm doing the best I can and that is good enough!

I have often heard people say they will not raise their children the way they were raised. I have to agree in certain instances because we should try not to repeat the same mistakes our parents made.

Each generation is different and what worked for one generation may not necessarily work for the next one. I do however believe in healthy discipline and strong values, and it must be instilled from a young age.

Children need a foundation from which to start building their own thinking and viewpoints.

Today, I'm proud of each of my three children and I make a point of letting them know. I make sure that they know they are loved and I support each new dream of theirs.

I encourage their need to explore and make new discoveries.

I see each new achievement as a sign from God that I'm doing the best I can and that is good enough!

 **VOYAGE**

> *"I think that the best thing we can do for our children is to allow them to do things for themselves, allow them to be strong, allow them to experience life on their own terms, allow them to take the subway . . . let them be better people, let them believe more in themselves."*
> – C. JoyBell C.

Being a committed parent takes exactly that – commitment.

To be able to take care of your children, you first need to take care of yourself.

You need to be able to stay in control so that you can be the patient and supportive parent your child deserves.

Being healthy and able to control your emotions (in spite of high stress levels) will help you engage with your child in a manner that they will feel safe and valued.

Show your child what love is by assuring them that you love them, warts and all. They will learn that unconditional love does exist and that they are loved for exactly who they are!

Your 'Sport Star' and your 'Actress' need to feel that you love them both the same way, even though they are completely different and unique.

Make time to connect as a family. Before rushing off to start busy days, make time to check that everyone is okay with the needs of the day ahead.

"Homework done?"

"Feeling confident about the test or the match or auditions in the afternoon?"

Assure them of your love and support. Start the day right! In the afternoon, when everyone's home, bathed and dressed for bed, sitting down for dinner, it is time to check in again. "How did your day go?" If you were able to be there for the match or the audition, discuss it. Ask how their friends are – this gives insight into their emotional state.

Teach your children respect by respecting them, and you will be rewarded with respect!

Teach your child their emotions are important, but also that they need to manage them. Allow them to express their emotions by assuring them of your support and love. If they cry, vent, laugh or rage, simply be with them in that moment.

> *Teach your children respect by respecting them, and you will be rewarded with respect!*

Forgive, guide and show gratitude. Children will and do misbehave because they are testing boundaries. When they push, it is because they are on unfamiliar territory. Then it is time to re-enforce your ground rules firmly, forgive the mistake (nobody is perfect and we all learn by making mistakes), guide them to the right way of doing things, and when they do them right, show gratitude.

Good behaviour and learning from mistakes should be rewarded. These lessons will last until adulthood, where learning from mistakes becomes extremely important.

RONÈL M HARRIS

"Death leaves a heartache no one can heal, love leaves a memory no one can steal."

– From an Irish headstone

CHAPTER 9

Death
Unforeseen

I fell asleep waiting for Leon to arrive home. I woke up with somebody knocking on the door. I heard cars stopping outside and I thought Leon had brought the party home. "He must have had one too many and his friends have brought him home." I opened the door with a big smile, but I saw only his friends. "Hello," I said, while still trying to wake up, "where is my husband?"

Two policemen stepped forward. One of them confirmed who I was and apologetically continued, "Sorry to bring you the bad news, but your husband was involved in an accident."

Let this be a nasty joke, please God, don't let this happen to me!

"Oh? Let me fetch my baby and I will go with you to the hospital."

As I turned around, he touched my elbow. "Sorry, Mrs. Rossouw, I don't think you understand . . ."

I was only 20 and a widow.

I stopped and slowly turned back. "Your husband died on the scene." He handed me Leon's wedding band. "He asked me, as he was dying: 'Please, give this to my Baby . . .'"

I ran outside, screaming manically. I opened car doors looking for him, crying out and calling his name. "Leon! Leon, where are you? Let this be a nasty joke, please God, don't let this happen to me! We've been married for only 18 months, it can't be true." I kept on running down the road until I stumbled and fell on the dirt. My knees were bruised and scratched from the gravel.

Someone tried to help me get up, but I wouldn't let anyone touch me. I allowed no one near me. I lashed out at God. "How could You do this to me? How could You give me someone to love and then just take him away? Just like that! Please God, please, tell me I am having a horrific dream!"

My baby was only four months old when a knock on the door changed my whole life. My world disintegrated. My dreams fragmented into desolate sorrow and wretched despair.

Leon was riding his motorbike down the road, now known as Beyers Naude Avenue. A taxi approached from an adjacent dirt road and ignored the stop sign, turning into Leon's lane. The taxi hit him. They would not let me see him because of the extent of the injuries he sustained.

As reality dawned and I could no longer deny the loss of my husband, I lost my mind and then I lost our unborn baby. The excruciating pain I experienced during the miscarriage was nothing compared to the agony in my heart.

I woke during the night and in the dim moonlight, I saw Leon standing at the bottom of the bed. It wasn't a dream . . . "What are you doing here? They told me you were dead!" I whispered, suddenly filled with hope that the whole terrible ordeal had been a nightmare, but knowing better.

He softly answered: "I am not dead, and I will always be here for you."

For a long time, I did not want to leave my room because it was the room where I saw Leon the night of his death. I could still feel his presence and every night, I could feel his arms around me holding me tightly.

I was only 20 and a widow. I did not know how I would cope with the tragedy of my beloved husband's death. Let alone raise our son alone. How was I going to raise our child without his father?

I can hardly remember the funeral and the weeks that followed. My parents-in-law had to put their own sadness of losing a son aside and they took care of baby Leon and I.

How do I describe my sorrow to you without sounding melodramatic? I cannot explain how severely damaged I was losing my beloved and my unborn baby the same night.

Words can never do justice for the feeling of devastation and loneliness I experienced. I felt lost and useless, and I saw no future. I felt broken, empty as if someone had ripped my heart from my chest. I was barely functioning. I isolated myself in our room. I felt that I would never be able to face the world again. I sank deeper into the darkest pit of depression.

> *"I feel honoured that I am able to fill your cracks with love. You and our son are my whole life... I will always love you..."*

Leon helped me discover a new me, the real me, but I was so closely bound to him that I didn't think I could be that person without him! I didn't think I could be anyone without him. My dreams were his dreams. His dreams were my dreams.

I had lost hope at one point in my life, but he restored my faith in men and love. I saw no future without him. He had walked into my life when I needed to be loved. Leon Rossouw loved me unconditionally.

I was so angry with God because for the first time in my life, He had given me someone who cared for me and never asked for anything in return, and He took him away.

Even now, after all these years, I can almost not believe what happened to me and how I survived it all. I often contemplated suicide – it felt like the only way I could be reunited with the man of my dreams. I did not want to accept that in the real life, our fairy tale, our "happily ever after", was not to be. The ultimate love story ended too soon.

I remembered how he stalled that fateful morning before he left; he did not want to leave us. The beautiful message he wrote on the mirror not knowing it would be his last.

"I feel honoured that I am able to fill your cracks with love. You and our son are my whole life . . . I will always love you . . ."

Suddenly, one day I felt claustrophobic between the four walls of the bedroom. I had to get out.

I took our son and got into the car. I started driving aimlessly. I did not know where I was going to or where I wanted to be. I put Leon's favourite song, "Islands in the Stream", on repeat.

I cried so hard, I couldn't see the road sometimes. I don't know how long or how far I drove – but all of a sudden, I realised it was dark. Seeing a light in the distance, I decided to drive on to find a suitable place to turn around. At first, I didn't pay much attention to the light in the distance, but as I came closer, I saw it was a man and he started waving his torch wildly at me. He was trying to warn me about something, but by the time I saw the oncoming train, it was too late.

I made a haphazard attempt to avoid hitting the train, but my foot slipped as I reached over to the passenger seat to protect baby Leon, and I accidentally hit the accelerator. I lost control of the car as it crashed into the side of the train but I managed to shield my baby with my body. Then I heard the terrible sounds of breaking glass, metal crashing into metal.

I later learned the car got hooked on a side ladder and was dragged along with the train, which prevented the train from dragging the car under it. We were spared from further harm by a tree growing next to the railway line, which obstructed the car. The car became unstuck and stopped next to the railway line.

I woke up in the hospital. I was vaguely aware of a nurse who told me I had been in an accident: "Nothing happened to your baby. He doesn't have a single scratch. He is safe and in good hands."

I closed my eyes and escaped into a deep sleep.

> *"Only people who are capable of loving strongly can also suffer great sorrow, but this same necessity of loving serves to counteract their grief and heals them."*
> – Leo Tolstoy

The Unreality Of Death

 ANCHOR

> "When someone you love dies, and you're not expecting it, you don't lose them all at once; you lose them in pieces over a long time – the way the mail stops coming, and their scent fades from the pillows and even from the clothes in their closet and drawers. Gradually, you accumulate the parts of them that are gone. Just when the day comes – when there's a particular missing part that overwhelms you with the feeling that they're gone, forever – there comes another day, and another specifically missing part."
>
> – John Irving, *A Prayer for Owen Meany*

When I was told my husband died, I immediately went into denial – it couldn't be! We were so happy. We had our whole life together waiting, our baby boy was only four months old and I was pregnant with another baby! Leon just got promoted! He couldn't just leave us like this! I did not want to hear I was never going to see my beautiful husband ever again.

In the days that followed, I functioned on autopilot, barely paying attention to anything or anyone around me. I stayed in bed. All I wanted to do was sleep, because when you are asleep, the world and the pain do not exist. I felt numb and listless.

I stopped living almost at the same time my husband did. Nothing and no one could awaken me from the deep dark state I was in. I did not want to talk to anyone or think about anything. I wanted nothing to do with the funeral arrangements. I didn't want to hear people talk about Leon.

I was not thinking straight when I put baby Leon in the car that afternoon; my only thought was that I needed to escape. I wanted to clear my head. I was lost in my memories when the accident happened.

I have only vague recollections of the incident – everything happened so fast.

Today, I am grateful that I can share my experiences with you and the lessons I learned. Dealing with the loss of a loved one is always traumatic, and because we are all different and unique individuals, we have different coping mechanisms. Nobody escapes the death of a beloved, and no one can ever be prepared for it.

> *I stopped living almost at the same time my husband did.*

 ## COMPASS

> *"Grief is a most peculiar thing; we're so helpless in the face of it. It's like a window that will simply open of its own accord. The room grows cold, and we can do nothing but shiver. But it opens a little less each time and a little less; and one day we wonder what has become of it."*
> – Arthur Golden, *Memoirs of a Geisha*

Because death and dying is an inevitable part of everyone's lives, research on loss and grief is ongoing.

The subject is particularly complicated because grief cannot be researched and presented along with generalized findings. Grief is a deeply personal emotion, unique to each individual, but understanding the phases one goes through after such an experience can help make the healing process more bearable.

Although the four phases or stages of grief have been identified, no one experiences every phase in the same way. You may move through the phases quicker or slower; you may move through them in a different order; you may skip a phase or task altogether. Your needs will instinctively be met in the way you have to resolve the grieving process.

The stages of grief can be divided into four distinct phases:

1. **Numbness** – immediately after the loss you experience a feeling of numbness, this is a defence mechanism that allows you to survive emotionally.

2. **Searching And Yearning** – also referred to as pining, characterized bylonging or yearning for the deceased to return. Emotions expressed during this time may include weeping, anger, anxiety and confusion.

3. **Disorganization And Despair** – withdrawal from people and social activities. Feelings of pining and yearning are replaced by apathy – meaning an absence of emotion and despair.

4. **Re-Organization And Recovery** – the final phase. You are slowly returning to 'normal'. Grief never ends but thoughts of sadness and despair are diminished while positive memories of the deceased take over.

My sense of loss and brokenness did not allow me to reach the last stage – I had a total mental collapse and only through intense therapy did I manage to resolve this.

Grief is a deeply personal emotion, unique to each individual.

 **VOYAGE**

> *"Deep grief sometimes is almost like a specific location, a coordinate on a map of time. When you are standing in that forest of sorrow, you cannot imagine that you could ever find your way to a better place. But if someone can assure you that they themselves have stood in that same place and now have moved on, sometimes this will bring hope."*
> – Elizabeth Gilbert, *Eat Pray Love*

From the research I have done, I have identified common (or similar) tools to which I related.

There are four 'tasks' of mourning one has to work through after experiencing loss. The term 'tasks' is used because it involves a considerable amount of effort and hard work:

ACCEPTING the reality that your loved one has died and will not return is the first task that needs to be completed. Without coming to terms with this, there is no forward movement in the process. Nothing else can happen before you accept the situation.

Grief is painful – physically and emotionally. It is important to ACKNOWLEDGE THE PAIN, and DON'T SUPPRESS IT.

> *You deserve to be free and you deserve to live the best life you possibly can.*

ADJUST to a new world your loved one is no longer part of. For example, your home and places that you used to visit together. This may also require adjusting the roles that the deceased played in your life. If your spouse died, it will require the acceptance of a new identity as a widow or widower, and single parent if there are children.

And the last step finally, is finding an appropriate place in your life for the memories. This requires LETTING GO OF THE EMOTIONAL ATTACHMENTS, and only then will you be able to start new relationships.

It is very important that you please remember this:

There is no timeline for these tasks; the duration and pace totally depends on you – as long as you do them.

If you can't manage the process by yourself, confide in a friend you trust or seek professional help.

You deserve to be free and you deserve to live the best life you possibly can.

Important note: Please remember that I am not a trained grief counsellor or therapist. As I pointed out before, my observations stem from my own personal experience. I was also prompted by my own suffering to assist others after the loss of a beloved to avoid following the same road of disaster I ended up on.

If you cannot cope with the loss of a loved one, please seek professional help immediately.

RONÈL M HARRIS

"When we least expect it, life sets us a challenge to test our courage and willingness to change; at such a moment, there is no point in pretending that nothing has happened or in saying that we are not yet ready. The challenge will not wait. Life does not look back. A week is more than enough time for us to decide whether or not to accept our destiny."

– Paulo Coelho,
The Devil and Miss Prym

CHAPTER 10

Fate Took My Hand

I don't know how long I was comatose, but when I woke up eventually, after seeing Leon in a dream, reaching out to touch his hand and pulling back because the coldness, it frightened me. I didn't want to wake up and I immediately felt nauseous – the pungent scent of disinfectant was overwhelming. It reminded me of the time I visited my mother in the Hillbrow hospital.

I tried to sit up but I was too weak.

I heard a distant voice asking: "Do you remember you were in an accident? Do you remember what happened?"

I tried to answer, but no words came from my mouth. I was desperate to know where my son was, but I could not talk. The harder I tried, the more exasperated I became. I was on the verge of hysteria. I wanted to scream, but could not. My lips were moving and I wanted to talk, but I just couldn't.

Everyone around my bed was just standing there, just staring at me. Not saying anything.

"Where is my son?" No sound, my agitation growing . . . no answers. By now I was becoming frantic.

A nurse injected me with a sedative and just before I fell into another deep sleep I heard her voice echoing from far away: "Relax, your baby boy is fine. Your family is looking after him. He is safe." Then her voice was loud and clear, "You have a broken collar bone but you will go home soon."

How did I get here, how did I let myself go this far? My screams ricocheted in my head.

I fell into a deep sleep again. I have no idea how long I slept, but when I woke up, I forced my eyes open. I vaguely remember short periods of waking, but I was adamant to keep them open this time. I wanted to see where I was and what was happening around me.

Battling to focus, I saw a woman sitting in the corner across from me, rocking backwards and forwards, mumbling inaudible sentences. Next to me, a woman was tugging violently at her hair, her eyes were fixed on a specific spot on the wall, as if nothing could divert her attention. I heard people crying and others screaming in other rooms. I could hear nurses trying to calm them.

Even in my disorientated state, I realised I was amongst people who were quite obviously mentally unwell. It baffled me that I was in the same ward. "I do not belong here," the thought kept repeating in my head. "I need to get home; I have a baby to look after!"

I had to go to the bathroom and I slowly got up from the hospital bed. I had no idea where the bathroom was, but I suddenly found myself walking down a long, dark corridor full of people sitting or standing around, all looking at me strangely.

I eventually found the bathroom where I was confronted by another woman. She looked gaunt and very pale; it looked like she hadn't brushed her hair in weeks. Her eyes – sunken deeply into her skull – were hardly noticeable, but I could see she was trying to look at me. Then all of sudden, she vanished – she was gone! I did not know if it was my imagination, so I walked back to the spot where I saw her. Suddenly, she was there again! Right in front of me. But this time, she didn't disappear into thin air. While staring at her, I slowly started realizing I was staring at myself in the mirror! I was horrified! I couldn't believe what I saw!

I moved my one hand up slowly and touched my face, my hair . . . yes! It was me! I was looking at my own image in the mirror!

I could not believe this was, in fact, me!

"How did this happen?" I asked myself over and over. I was overcome with fear, I started breathing faster; how did I get here, how did I let myself go this far? My screams ricocheted in my head.

"Please no! Please God, help me!" The louder I screamed on the inside, the more desperate I became. There were still no sounds coming from my mouth. I sank down on my knees and screamed the same sentence over and over. "Please no! Please God, help me!"

Suddenly, without any warning, my words echoed and ricochet in the empty bathroom! Thank God! My voice was back and I made sure everyone in the hospital could hear my despair! My screaming woke up the whole ward and by the time the nurses got to me, I was uncontrollable. When they tried to touch me, I started kicking! They had to physically restrain me to sedate me. When I woke up the next morning, I realised it was not all a bad dream.

A few days later, I had calmed down and accepted that I really been admitted to a mental institution. I still couldn't believe that I had sunk so low, but I knew that I was willing to do anything to get myself out of there and get back home to my son.

I needed help. Desperately.

Early one morning, a nurse came for me. She took me to another wing and told me to wait in a long queue. "Wait here for your turn to see the doctor." I was very nervous waiting for my appointment. I had no idea what to expect. My head was spinning and I felt sick. Then finally, my name was called. It was my turn. I could almost not get up from the chair.

The doctor was ready to see me.

I felt faint when I walked through the door into the office where this big man sat behind his big desk. I suddenly felt very small in a big office. He did not smile when he pointed towards a chair and told me to sit down. He was almost business-like when he started talking to me, but as he continued, I started calming down.

He was very sympathetic when he started to explain everything to me – what happened to me and everything they observed since I was brought to the psychiatric ward. At the end of our consultation, I realised I was in big trouble.

I needed help. Desperately.

I had no choice but to cooperate because I wanted to go home, back to my baby. I wanted to be a good mother to my son. I wanted to get my life back on track again.

"How could I forget the promises I made to myself so many years ago? Whatever happened to Scarlett O'Hara?"

My treatment started the very next day. The doctor assisted me every step of the way as I slowly started working through all the pain and grief of my past. I had to recover all those memories I tucked far away, hoping they would all disappear as time went by. It was extremely painful to explore my past and get to the root of all the hurt and suffering.

Sometimes, it became almost too much to bear, but I knew it was something I had to do if I wanted to be a well-adjusted person to achieve my dreams. I had no other option if I wanted to be reunited with my son and be a good mother to baby Leon.

I lost myself and betrayed my dreams. I kept on repeating the same question in my mind: "How could I forget the promises I made to myself so many years ago? Whatever happened to Scarlett O'Hara?"

For the first time, I spoke freely about everything. My father, my mother, Richard, picking up coal, everything . . . every detail. While undergoing treatment, I learned it was impossible to erase my past from my subconscious – it was always there, simmering, waiting to boil over. I could not suppress the shock of Leon's death. I could not fall back on burying my pain, and I fell into the grave I dug myself.

My psychiatrist had to use hypnotherapy to uncover all the experiences I buried away – the only way I could survive. I tried to wipe out all the pain and suffering of my past by banning all the unresolved issues of my childhood into the darkest of places. I took a vow that I would never revisit those terrible years or remember the sexual abuse my father subjected me to, his violent behaviour and the poverty of my youth.

The psychiatrist recorded everything while I was under hypnosis and afterwards, he played it back to me. I came face to face with all the memories I thought I had wiped out forever. I don't know how I coped. I had to relive every moment I had 'erased' from my life and never talked about – I could not even share it with Leon. I was confronted with all the hurt, the pain, humiliation, abuse and rejection – there was no backdoor. I could not escape any more. My survival mechanism had led to my breakdown and I collapsed. I had to come to terms with all those memories I had run away from. Only then I could heal and become a full person – for the first time in my life.

I was present when my godmother listened to the recordings. My godmother never forgot my frantic attempt to confide in her. When I told her of my father's abuse, she chose to dismiss it. I watched her, seeing the pain she was feeling on her face. Not to mention the guilt. She realised she could've saved me, but she preferred to turn a blind eye. It was much easier than uncovering and facing my father's wickedness. The terrible truth of child abuse was a taboo subject then, especially if it happened on your own doorstep. It was the case then, and it is still the case.

> *I knew I needed tools to cope with the future. I could not afford another breakdown; I knew I had to be strong.*

She was floored and apologetic, but she knew the damage was done. It was too late to be sorry, but I could not waste my energy on negative emotions such as resentment and hatred. I had to concentrate on my own healing.

I did not know how I was going to do it, but I knew I had to accept Leon belonged to the past. Our marriage had been almost too good to be true; I felt safe. Losing that security left me vulnerable. I had no confidence. I would have to find work but it was not going to be easy. I had no self-esteem. I had to find a place to live but I had no money, no income. I would be leaving Sterkfontein Hospital soon to embark on my new life. Alone, without Leon. I knew I needed tools to cope with the future. I could not afford another breakdown; I knew I had to be strong. I owed it to my son . . . to me, we deserved a good life, the best life. I would not deprive him as I was deprived.

After confronting and working through all my childhood experiences, I knew I could put the past where it belonged – in the past – not run away from it like before. But I did not have to be haunted anymore by scary images accompanied by the soundtrack of his voice, whispering: "Now you don't tell Mommy anything – this is our secret? You understand? If you do, you know what will happen to Mommy and you don't want that."

On my road to recovery, I accepted the fact that I couldn't do anything about my past. It was over. I could not undo or change the damage of my childhood, but I did not need to nurture it. The biggest breakthrough was learning that I was not to be blamed for the molestation – it was not my fault!

I could only control my present and I had a choice. I had the choice to start living my life to the fullest. Only I could make that choice; I had to own it. I chose to embrace life.

I was discharged almost eight weeks later. I could not wait to see my baby again. Climbing into the car and seeing him in the back seat, I knew I would never allow myself to lose control like this again. I was scared. I didn't know what my future held, but I was determined. Looking back at the hospital slowly fading into the distance, my thoughts were interrupted by a song on the radio, "Papilon" by George Baker, about a butterfly breaking free from its cocoon.

As I was listening to the words, tears were running down my cheeks, but they were tears of relief and tears of hope. The song became symbolic of my new life and that I had been able to break free from a past filled with hurt, fear and sadness.

> *"We delight in the beauty of the butterfly but rarely admit the changes it has gone through to achieve that beauty."*
> – Maya Angelou

Emerging From The Chrysalis

 ANCHOR

> *"Fate is never fair. You are caught in a current much stronger than you are; struggle against it and you'll drown not just yourself, but those who try to save you. Swim with it and you'll survive."*
>
> – Cassandra Clare, *City of Ashes*

When I was finally and completely awake from my coma, I had to face the harsh reality of what I had let myself become. The face I saw in the mirror and the helplessness and hopelessness I saw in that woman's eyes was horrifying to say the least.

Gone was the happy, carefree, passionate woman that I once was, and in her place was this broken, tired, listless woman devoid of emotion – it was like looking at a stranger in the mirror. My car accident and the events that followed mercifully brought me exactly where I needed to be – the psychiatric ward, where I would get the help that I desperately needed.

> *My car accident and the events that followed mercifully brought me exactly where I needed to be - the psychiatric ward, where I would get the help that I desperately needed.*

It's strange how things work out, isn't it? You don't realise that the universe is conspiring to force you to take a good hard look at your life, to resolve your issues, be it things that happened in your past or by stopping you if you are on a collision course and need to change direction.

I have come to realise that nothing in life happens without a reason.

Whether the reason may be to change the course you are heading or to completely change your direction, you need to follow the current and not resist. Coming face to face with a past that I thought I had buried so deep was excruciatingly painful to say the least. In dealing with the pain of losing my beloved Leon and then setting myself free from the shackles that kept me prisoner, I was finally able to reclaim my life and start becoming the woman I was meant to be.

 ## COMPASS

> "No one saves us but ourselves. No one can and no one may. We ourselves must walk the path."
> – Gautama Buddha

Admitting you need help is not a sign of weakness, but rather a sign of courage. Always remember that no one can force you to break down the walls you are hiding behind, but the right people will make you want to do it yourself.

Being anchored in your past or in un-forgiveness keeps you from being able to become the person you were destined to be.

Being anchored in your past or in un-forgiveness keeps you from being able to become the person you were destined to be. You have an obligation to yourself to set yourself free from whatever it is that is holding you back.

- Is an unresolved issue anchoring you?
- Are you able to break the hold it has on you?
- Do you think it's time you sought help to resolve it?

It took Leon's death and the accident to get me the help that I needed to fully come to terms with my painful past.

You need to start being honest with yourself.

In the chapter you've just read, I learned it was impossible to erase my past – it was always there, simmering just under the surface, waiting to boil over. I could not suppress the shock of Leon's death. I could not resort to burying my pain; I had fallen into a grave I dug myself.

 **VOYAGE**

> *"Sometimes you imagine that everything could have been different for you, that if only you had gone right one day when you chose to go left, you would be living a life you could never have anticipated. But at other times you think there was no other way forward – that you were always bound to end up exactly where you have."*
>
> – Kevin Brockmeier, *The View from the Seventh Layer*

Think about your answers in the COMPASS section.

- What is keeping you from setting yourself free from the burdens you are carrying on your shoulders? Is it too painful? Do you feel that you are not strong enough as a person?
- Are you afraid of dealing with the problem because that may mean confronting old memories or maybe a person who has wronged you in some way?
- Are you not acknowledging the issues because you have buried them thinking they will go away by themselves?
- What is keeping you from seeking help? Is it embarrassment or the fear of being judged or ridiculed?

You need to start being honest with yourself.

I want to tell you that had it not been for the fact that I was in the hospital and then moved to the psychiatric ward, where I received the help that I needed, I most likely would not have sought help because I was always the strong one, the one who held everything and everyone together up until that stage. I most likely would have carried on the way I always did. But I do realise that the unresolved issues in our lives have a way of resurfacing over and over again until they are properly dealt with.

Whatever your answers to the previous questions, you need to realise one very important thing . . .

You are stopping yourself from reaching your full potential as a human being, as a partner to your significant other, as a parent to your children, even as a friend to others.

There is a whole part of your being that you are keeping locked away from the world. There is a whole person in each and every one of us, and you owe it to yourself more than anyone else to fully and completely embrace that person. The only way you will be able to reach for your dreams and fulfil your destiny is by shaking off the shackles that are keeping you prisoner.

> *"There is always a butterfly that exists in all of us, from the day we are born there exists this magical transformation in all that we do breathe and even fear . . . where it molds us to the magnificent and unique beings that we become till the day we are reborn."*
> – Angie Karan Krezos

"It is not because things are difficult that we do not dare – it's because we do not dare that things are difficult."

– Seneca

CHAPTER 11

Back To Work

My collapse following Leon's death was a milestone, a major turning point in my life. Once I was better, I realised how selfish my actions were. I had stopped fighting, but I owed it to my son to get back up. It was not easy; it took many years for me to get where I am today. I took baby steps.

Reunited with my darling baby boy, we were living with Leon's parents but being with them reminded me too much of Leon, and I had to get away from that. I started making plans but I had no illusions; I knew striking out on my own spelled hard times. I had nothing except for my clothes and I did not have much money at all, but I decided to move to Alberton anyway.

I rented a one-bedroom flat, furnished with only a mattress on the floor. I bought a piece of furniture every month. My first priority was my son's room. I asked my godparents to take care of him during the week and without hesitation, they agreed. I did not know it at the time, but they were about to file for divorce. They decided to wait and look after my baby while I found my feet.

Whenever I think of this selfless act, I am overcome with love and respect. They put their own future happiness on hold when they saw how determined I was to make the best of my life.

It was sad to be separated from my boy, to only see him on weekends. He was growing up fast, but I knew I was not yet ready to take on my role as mother – either financially or emotionally.

My new job as a debt collector was not particularly stimulating, but at least I had an income and I was slowly getting back into a routine, the discipline of everyday life. I had to walk to work and back, and although it was good exercise and afforded me time to think and daydream, it was a happy day when I received an unexpected windfall of money that was paid out to me from The Road Accident Fund (from the third-party claim that was lodged after Leon's accident). I used it to buy a small car and more furniture.

They put their own future happiness on hold when they saw how determined I was to make the best of my life.

I was starting to feel good about myself; my confidence was building again – slowly but surely. It was time to move on and I was open to any opportunities. I applied for a few vacancies and I was called for an interview. The position was that of a secretary at one of the big banks. I was so nervous as it was my first corporate interview in years.

I was appointed! The new position earned me enough money to have my son come home to live with me. This new challenge was exactly the injection I needed. I always wanted more from life. Gradually, my ambitious nature surfaced again and I started dreaming like before. I still felt lost and lonely at times, but I was getting stronger and I was ready to take on more challenges.

Actively cultivating a positive attitude, I found inspiration in reading about people who conquered life in spite of all the odds stacked against them. Simple messages of hope and encouraging quotations contributed to my new way of thinking. Reading and sharing these messages and quotations made me feel good. It bolstered my quest for optimism – it was a helpful tool. I felt more motivated every day; my sense of self-worth was renewed.

I was happy with my position at the bank and the stable income it provided for the moment, but I dreamed of having my own business, of being in control of my own life, my time, and my finances. Unfortunately, I did not have the necessary training to start one, but I was not going to let that stand in my way. I kept an open mind, knowing that once I came across the right opportunity, I would recognise it.

It came to me quite unexpected one day: I was walking at the centre near my office and saw a small store TO LET, and the idea just dropped – a small fashion store! I always dreamed about a career in fashion, but I thought it to be a pipe-dream. The shop would be ideal for a little boutique. I could already visualize beautiful dresses displayed in the window. I spent each night daydreaming and putting plans in place, trying to figure out how I could turn this dream into a reality.

> *I ruled out any possibility of another romantic relationship because I was definitely not going to get hurt again, but we became the best of friends.*

I made an enquiry at the landlord's about the rent and deposit – I didn't have that kind of money! I spent my evenings and weekends working on my dream, knowing that I would need to research every avenue thoroughly to work out how I could make this happen.

I made an appointment with the landlord and I told them about my plans for the store and, after presenting my research, managed to prove to them that my fashion store would be a success and they allowed me to take occupation. I had to pay a small deposit to have my shop fitted though and agreed to pay the outstanding balance within 90 days. I had no money for stock so I contacted and convinced a few designers to give me garments on appro. I had even decided on a name for my shop and my enthusiasm about my new venture was contagious. No one was more excited than me, though. Although I had no experience or training, I was going to become the owner of my own business at the tender age of 22!

Dramatic change was afoot on a personal level too. I was waiting for a bus home one afternoon while I was still working my notice period at the bank. That was when I met Riaan – very friendly, he introduced himself to me. As we chatted, we discovered we worked for the same company. I was shy at first. I did not socialize much. I spent every spare minute with my son, making up for lost time, but Riaan had such an easy manner that he soon made me feel comfortable enough to want to spend more time with him. We spent our lunch breaks during that last month together. I told him about my business and realised the centre was not far from where he lived.

> *I became addicted to success. Soon, I was spending most of my time at work or going to functions and less time at home.*

I ruled out any possibility of another romantic relationship because I was definitely not going to get hurt again, but we became the best of friends. In spite of my resolve, Riaan slowly grew on me. I was attracted to his honest and caring temperament. I did not have any other friends so we saw each other frequently, and I invited him to meet my son. They caught on like a house on fire! I realised then that my son needed a male figure to identify with. He was a good man who came from a good family.

Riaan invited us to join him for a visit at his parents' place and I connected with them right away. His father was a gentle, caring man, and I admired his stepmother for her elegance and her dress sense. It was a family I could happily be a part of. They embraced me unconditionally and with the warmth I never knew as a child. I started feeling contented with Riaan. My son liked him and when he proposed to me a few months later, it felt like the right thing to do. I had doubts; no one could replace my beloved Leon, but I wasn't going to forego an opportunity to love and be happy again.

A week or two before our wedding, Leon appeared to me in a dream. He walked me down the aisle and gave me away to Riaan. Nodding to him, Leon asked him to be a good father to young Leon and then he told Riaan to treasure me as his new wife. When I woke up the next morning, I knew I had Leon's blessing. I believed his spirit was with me all the time. He was always close – like he promised.

Riaan and I had the most beautiful wedding. Everything was planned exactly the way I always dreamed it. I wore an exquisite wedding dress and I know I looked absolutely beautiful when I walked down the aisle to start this new chapter in my life.

I had a stable, loving home and I relished being a part of the fashion world. Soon, I felt it was time for the next challenge. My prospect this time was in the beauty and slimming industry. I opened a slimming salon and even though life was hectic managing two businesses, I really enjoyed the thrill of being busy, celebrating milestones with my clients seeing their results. I was in my element amongst people in the middle of the action.

I became addicted to success. Soon, I was spending most of my time at work or going to functions and less time at home. I was taken in by a world in which I met a lot of like-minded, successful people, and I thrived among them. I was a contributing member of the commerce industry. On the flip-side, I became a little self-obsessed and started to neglect my family. While I learned a lot about myself during the whole process, I had yet to learn about the importance of balance.

Riaan knew I was never going to be a housewife again. I revelled in my independence. Leon did not see much of me, but I knew he was happy and cared for. Riaan enjoyed staying at home while I flourished socialising. I became the person I always wanted to be: Confident, strong and driven. I was capable of achieving anything if I put my mind to it. I would never doubt myself again.

Riaan loved me and he understood why I was so driven, but I don't think he expected me to change so much. I could not deny that I was overlooking my duties as a wife and to a lesser degree, I was not fulfilling my role as a mother either. I made time to spend with my son, playing with him and making sure he was doing well and all his needs were met, but I also needed to be there for him emotionally. He was, nevertheless, a confident young man, blessed with all the love and security I never had.

My marriage was waning. I never questioned Riaan's love or commitment, but I knew my feelings were no longer the same. I felt guilty because he was a truly wonderful man who doted on my son and understood and accepted my needs, but something was missing. I started enjoying the attention of other men. I never allowed anything to develop but I had thoughts.

One man in particular often walked past my shop, looking at me. At first I pretended not to notice him. I was a married woman and even if were single, I have to admit that I once (laughing to myself) thought, "He's too short for me!"

He walked left instead of right one day, straight into my shop as I was sitting doing my books, and he cockily announced: "You are going to be my wife one day." I just laughed it off, replying: "You don't have what it takes!" He introduced himself as John and we became friends. After a while he also became friends with Riaan, and Leon started taking kickboxing lessons from him.

I realised I was looking for things to keep me busy and away from home. It confused me because I could not understand why I was avoiding my husband. Why didn't I want to be alone with him? How could I not be happy?

I was married to a man who bought me a new car every year as a Valentine's Day gift; not brand-new, but a definite improvement. I was married to a man who spoiled me with bunches of fresh flowers, a man who treated me with the utmost respect and, above all, he was an adoring father to my son. I realised that I was feeling guilty for neglecting them and when I was home, I tried to make up for it by cooking them special meals. I have always loved cooking and I was sincere when I tried to spoil them with one of my creative concoctions.

I tried not to let anyone notice my loneliness. In spite of being around people who cared for me, I felt an empty void within me. I dismissed it – in my mind I was acting like an ungrateful teenager and I had to grow up.

I worked even harder in a bid to run from my troubling thoughts. I avoided what I actually felt . . . The consequences were too unpleasant to contemplate.

Picking Up My Life – Again

 ANCHOR

> *"Never surrender your hopes and dreams to the fateful limitations others have placed on their own lives. The vision of your true destiny does not reside within the blinkered outlook of the naysayers and the doom prophets. Judge not by their words, but accept advice based on the evidence of actual results. Do not be surprised should you find a complete absence of anything mystical or miraculous in the manifested reality of those who are so eager to advise you. Friends and family who suffer the lack of abundance, joy, love, fulfillment and prosperity in their own lives really have no business imposing their self-limiting beliefs on your reality experience."*
>
> – Anthon St. Maarten, *Living a Life of Increase*

The hardest step of all and also the most important is to ADMIT to yourself that you are not where you want to or even should be!

Hitting rock-bottom was the most terrifying thing that could have happened to me. At the same time, it was of the utmost importance that I had to live through it. I discovered the inner fighter in me again! Picking up the pieces of your life AGAIN or making a radical change is hard, but there are a few guidelines to smooth the way. I learned them the hard way and I am confident that I can guide you.

The hardest step of all and also the most important is to ADMIT to yourself that you are not where you want to or even should be! Without this, you will not be able to pick yourself out of the rut you find yourself in.

 ## COMPASS

Just do it – stop making excuses or telling yourself that you can't – you have the power and the responsibility to make changes to your life at any point. If you don't like where you are, work to change it. It is not going to happen by itself.

Don't listen to what other people are saying if you feel that they are being negative or are projecting their own fears onto you. There will always be people around you who will listen to you and their faces will express the horror they feel when you tell them about something drastically different that you want to do. You can choose to take on their fear or to set it aside.

 ## VOYAGE

> *"Well, I always know what I want. And when you know what you want, you go toward it. Sometimes you go very fast and sometimes only an inch a year. Perhaps you feel happier when you go fast. I don't know. I've forgotten the difference long ago, because it really doesn't matter, so long as you move."*
>
> – Ayn Rand, *We the Living*

There are thousands of self-help websites that offer advice on how to start over, but it all boils down to a few different types of 'starting-overs', and each one is uniquely different with a 'personality' of their own. I will give you my interpretation, keeping it simple.

The "Let It Die To Grow"
In essence this means letting go of the parts of us that are hindering our growth. Just like a rosebush needs to be pruned in order for it to grow stronger and wield more roses, so do we. Cut whatever does not add value out of your life and grow.

The "My Choice"
This is the easiest type of starting over. You've decided what needs to be done, you have figured out a way to get it done, and you happily put the plan into action to make it happen – as simple as that.

The "It's Going To Be Awesome"
So you made goals and you had dreams, and after years of hard work, all your puzzle pieces suddenly starts falling into place and you have the opportunity to live the life, start the job or embark on the adventure you have worked so hard for. This type of change, though scary, is full of excitement and you realise that all your sacrifices have brought you to this new chapter in your life, and you can't wait to start it!

> *Here is where your courage, determination and perseverance will be put to the test!*

The "I Don't Want To, You Can't Make Me, I'm Going To Put It Off Until I Absolutely Have No Other Choice But To"
This one – being forced because you have no other choice – is the hardest of all the beginnings. It is hard because in your head and your heart, you may not be ready – BUT YOU HAVE TO – so you resist as long as you can, stubbornly hanging on. It might be saying goodbye to a bad habit, or committing to end a toxic relationship. Here is where your courage, determination and perseverance will be put to the test! For this new start to be successful, to close that door, you need to have the same courage, determination, perseverance and FAITH in yourself to open another.

DREAMS – COURAGE – PERSEVERANCE – DETERMINATION – FAITH

The best way to stay on course and have stability in your life is by setting 'personal', or rather, 'life' goals.

Consider what it is that you want to achieve in your life:

- **Career** – What level do you want to achieve? How can you do it?
- **Finance** – What do you need to earn and how does that tie in with your career plans?
- **Education** – What extra skills do you need to need to reach Career and Finance?
- **Family** – Do you want to be a parent or if you are already, what kind of parent do you want to be? How do you want to be seen by your family and or extended family?
- **Hobbies** – Do you have any interests that you would like to develop further?
- **Physical Or Health** – If you want to live a healthier lifestyle, what do you need to do? What do you need in order to accomplish this goal?
- **Social** – Do you need to make new social connections with more like-minded people who have the same interests as you? Are you able to attend more functions or events that will enable networking?

You can start by combining one sentence on each of these goals into your own "personal mission statement."

"Some changes look negative on the surface, but you will soon realize that space is being created in your life for something new to emerge."

– Eckart Tolle

CHAPTER 12

Will It *Ever* Stop?

My marriage was failing. I did not know or understand what caused my ardour to wane. It was another obstruction about to mar our existence.

Riaan and I were busy with household chores when the phone rang late one afternoon. I thought it would be work-related, thus I was somewhat reluctant to answer it.

"Yes, I am Ronèl, why?" It was a nurse from some hospital and when she explained why she was calling, I knew I should not have answered. She was acting on behalf of my father – he was a patient. I was speechless, staggered.

"You are his daughter, am I right?"

"Ye . . . yes?"

I had no idea how I would react upon seeing him again, but I did know for sure that I was a lot stronger and I was no longer frightened of him.

"I need to inform you that he was in a terrible accident a few months ago. He lost his leg, broke his pelvis and his arm is badly damaged. I must warn you he is not doing too well, but there is not much we can do for him here anymore. He is ready to be released, but he says he has nowhere to go . . ."

I felt the blood draining from my body. I just stood there holding the phone in my hand. I couldn't believe that he reappeared to foul up my life again! Why was it happening to me?

I told them I would arrange with someone in the family who may be able to help. He was not coming into my home! The idea of him invading my space was unthinkable.

Early in our relationship, I had told Riaan everything about my past and now, at a time when I could least afford putting more strain on our marriage, my father pops up out of nowhere. Just like with Leon, he was invading my life again.

When Riaan walked into the room, it was evident that something was very wrong; I was just standing there still holding the phone. I tried to stay calm. I was fighting the clamour of conflict raging inside.

"My father was in an accident and he is ready to be discharged from hospital. I just spoke with a nurse from there."

Riaan did not say anything while I phoned my sisters. Both of them said it was impossible for them to fetch him. He just stood there knowing how hard that was for me, how I was feeling.

It had fallen to me to step up once again. After an intense discussion, a lot of soul-searching and another call from the nurse, we left for the hospital. I had no idea how I would react upon seeing him again, but I did know for sure that I was a lot stronger and I was no longer frightened of him.

The first thing I noticed walking into his room was that he was a lot smaller than I remembered. It was clear that life did not treat him well. He looked old and frail, much older than his 57 years at that stage, but as soon as he opened his mouth, I knew he was still the same contemptible man – years of hardship and pain did not change him for the better.

"Are you taking your Daddy home with you?"

I looked at him and silently begged God to give me the strength to cope with having him in my house, having to look after him – to look at him every day!

When we arrived home, I set the rules of my house immediately. It provided me with a sense of control; of having power over him. "Keep your distance, stay away from my son and don't go anywhere near my room. If you even try to touch me, you are no longer welcome!" I had to set boundaries even if it seemed cruel. "If you respect my rules, you can stay until you are better. If you drink, you will have to leave!"

We did whatever we could to speed up his recovery – the sooner he got better, the sooner I could be rid of him. I was not spending much time at home before anyway, but I positively hated going home knowing he was there. I could not handle listening to him while he tried to make conversation with Riaan.

"Did you have a good day?" I wanted to vomit when he asked me how my day was; whenever he spoke to me. I had to contain my aversion when I heard him talking to my son. Slowly, his health was improving. I couldn't wait for him to leave. I wanted him out of my life! I started thinking of ways to prepare him; soon he would have to take care of himself.

> *"I don't care about your remorse, whether it is real or not. I will never forgive you." I left the room without looking back.*

I came home one evening to find him drunk and maudlin – somehow he had gotten into the liquor cabinet. From where I stood listening in the kitchen, I could hear him berating himself. Full of self-reproach and self-pity, he mumbled how desperately he wanted me to forgive him. He kept saying how we could both find peace if I would just listen to him. I wanted to explode! He was blaming me for the discord between us.

"God has punished me enough, but she still holds the past dangling over my head – like an axe." I could hardly make sense of his slurring, but I didn't want to hear any more anyway.

I don't know how I managed, but I stayed calm and collected. I did not want to create a scene in front of my son. I walked up to him and without raising my voice I said, emphasizing every word: "Take the car we had converted for you, pack your suitcase and when I get back from work tomorrow, you will be gone. I told you before and I'm telling you again for the last time, I will never forgive you. You ruined your families' lives – my mother's, my brothers' and sisters' lives and mine. I don't care about your remorse, whether it is real or not. I will never forgive you." I left the room without looking back.

When I arrived home the next day he was gone, along with several items he stole to sell for cash – I was, however, too grateful that he was gone to be angry because of that. My relief did not last very long. Just after midnight, the phone rang.

A sergeant from John Vorster Square was on the line. "Your father has just handed himself over for child molestation. He says you are the complainant and we need to speak to you to open a case."

Of course, he was still drunk. "Lock him up and throw away the key for all I care!" I was livid. He was trying to destroy me. We dropped Leon off with my in-laws and drove to the police station. I was beset by something impenetrably dark and it scared me. Riaan tried to calm me down, but the moment I walked into the interrogation room where he was regurgitating his drunken rubbish, I lost all composure. I clamped my hands around his throat and pushed him up against the wall. The policemen tried to pull me off of him, while Riaan was pleading with me to let go.

"Come on, baby, it is not worth it."

"Oh, yes it is!" I could see the blood draining from his face. His eyes dared me to finish him off, begging me to end his miserable life. He couldn't handle being an invalid so he resorted to baiting me – he hoped I would release him. Calculating as he ever was.

I slowly pulled my hands away from his throat. I would not give him this victory. He was not going to take my dignity from me. I heard myself shouting: "You are not going to do this to me! You will not force me to revisit your disgusting deeds in court, do you hear me?"

"Do you want to press charges, ma'am?"

"No and if he ever comes here again, don't bother phoning me!"

I could hardly breathe. I turned around and walked away from the pathetic creature sitting on the floor, crying like a baby!

"Please, please forgive me!"

I could still hear him as we stepped outside. I was more adamant than ever: "Never. I will never forgive you!"

The events of that night took an unmistakable toll on me. I had reached the end of my tether. Riaan tried to convince me that God would see justice done. "If you forgive him, you will feel so much better – lighter. You will be able to leave him behind and move on with your life." I just looked at him, thinking: "Can't you understand that I have moved on with my life? I have changed my life for the better! Why do I have to forgive him? How can anyone expect that of me?"

Soon, my father's intrusion into our lives became history, but like bad news, he kept making headlines. He disappeared for a while and then I received a message that he had been arrested. He mistook one of the workers on the smallholding where he lived for an intruder and he shot him. He was charged with murder but was found guilty of manslaughter and sentenced to five years in prison.

When I saw him in jail, I could not ignore the bleak state he was in, however much I despised him. He was defeated. I supplied him with toiletries and cigarettes and I paid money into his account so that he could buy protection; so that he could bribe fellow inmates. I even visited him as regularly as I could.

My mother was not doing well either. She was living with her boyfriend and drinking partner. I did not visit her often. Apparently, she was drinking more than ever in spite of having suffered three strokes. She phoned me only when she needed money, but I stopped giving it to her.

Although I did not really have love or respect for my mother, I still did not like seeing her health deteriorating. Every time I did visit, she was looking worse. It saddened and angered me at the same time. I had stopped trying to talk some sense into her brandy-soiled mind. I did not understand why she would stay with a man who was not looking after her, a man who kept on buying her alcohol, knowing very well every drink could be her last. I had given up – she could only help herself. Then she had her fifth, major stroke; the doctors informed us that she lost almost 25% of her brain function.

The stress of dealing with my parents, along with a troubled marriage, affected my health. I was diagnosed with both epilepsy and asthma, and was medicated accordingly. The anti-convulsive drug I was prescribed was known to cause depression and suicidal tendencies, along with several other side-effects.

Leon resented me for divorcing Riaan, and he found it difficult to forgive me. I was hindering father and son, stifling their relationship.

I was already struggling to hold my head above water and the medication was exacerbating my psychological anguish. It was as though there was a different person living inside my body. I became moody and volatile; swinging back and forth as if I was balancing on a pendulum. I was myself one minute, happy and comfortable in my skin, then suddenly I became angry and aggressive, outraged!

Riaan and I finally came to the conclusion that our marriage was over. There was no point in denying it any longer. I still admired Riaan – he was a good man who wanted only to have a family, something I wanted too, but after six miscarriages, a result of damage caused by the physical abuse of my childhood, we stopped trying. We had also lost our house – Riaan lost his job unexpectedly due to department shuffling, and he couldn't find new employment right away, which placed us under severe financial strain, further contributing to my declining feelings for him to some degree; I kept trying to understand why I could not love him as I should, but alas, we parted as friends.

Our son, then only 9 years old, suffered the most. He was informed of his biological father, of course, but Riaan was the only father he knew. He legally adopted Leon and raised him as his own. Riaan cared for him deeply and he was an exemplary parent, often standing in for me when I was absent because I spent my time living life in the fast lane. Leon resented me for divorcing Riaan, and he found it difficult to forgive me. I was hindering father and son, stifling their relationship.

I never explained that it was a mutual decision, although it often caused tension between us, especially when we found ourselves in less than ideal circumstances later. He could not see the reason in my actions – why did I give up a stable and secure life and choose to lead an existence in which nothing was guaranteed? Though we never wanted for anything, and all of our needs were always met, we often found ourselves on shaky ground. I did not have an answer then and I don't think I have one today.

Riaan currently works as our accountant with John and myself. With us. He lives near Leon and we all often go on holidays together. My son says Riaan knows me better than anyone; that he knows exactly how to handle me – he thinks the difficult times I faced after divorcing Riaan formed the backbone of the woman I am today. I don't know if that is true, but I feel blessed knowing that today we are one big happy family.

When the divorce was finalized, I sold my businesses, packed all of our belongings into my car and left. I had decided to indulge in a sabbatical, but it was a half-cocked, impulsive decision if I was to be perfectly honest – it stemmed from exhaustion. I was weary of responsibility, of budgets, stock and difficult clients and of disastrous relationships.

I only had my son to look after and I decided to take my ailing mother with us. I might not have been so gung-ho about it if a dear friend of many years, Ann, wasn't also joining us. She still is one of my best friends and because she knew me so well, she had the foresight to see that I was making a mistake. But headstrong like always, I maintained it was my turn to be a free spirit.

Although I became a rather nasty person, I still had friends who cared about me, like Ann, but instead of appreciating them, they made me feel claustrophobic.

We settled in Amanzimtoti, a small town on the coast of Kwa-Zulu Natal. It was a popular holiday destination. I booked a stand in a caravan park and paid for a whole year. Then I bought a park home and that was where we lived. I didn't have any plans because for once, I didn't have to. I liked the idea of being a hippie. I started wearing loose flowing dresses with flat sandals and long feathery earrings. I had to look the part!

The longer we were there, the more disconnected I became from everyone and everything. All I did was sleep and fight with everyone around me. I became impossible to live with. Although I became a rather nasty person, I still had friends who cared about me, like Ann, but instead of appreciating them, they made me feel claustrophobic. They were worried about the epilepsy and I resented being watched all the time. It made me feel like I was trapped in a cage!

My mood swings became unbearable and I became frustrated with my incongruous temperament. I couldn't deal with it on my own because I never had any privacy or a moment to myself; at least, that is how I perceived it then.

One evening, I went to have a bath. I needed to be alone. Ann became worried when she noticed I had been in the bathroom for a very long time. She came to check on me but realised the door was locked. She called my name and knocked. I didn't respond. She instinctively knew something was wrong so she mustered her strength to break down the door. She found me just in time. I had had a seizure and I could've drowned. I had no recollection of the incident.

Prone to angry outbursts, bouts of aching sadness or retreating into silence, I had no control over my emotions or my frame of mind. I felt guilty because I felt like I wasn't a good mother and I started drinking heavily. Waking up in the morning with a bottle of sparkling wine and going to bed with another only exaggerated my depression. I was feeling hopeless. The thought of ending my life – committing suicide – came up more and more regularly. I started believing that my son would be better off living with Riaan anyway. My marriage had failed, my mother needed my help to care for her, my father who kept resurfacing in my life, my epilepsy and the mood swings – all these things weighed me down so heavily. I felt like a complete and utter failure, unable to control my own life, let alone take care of my son.

One evening, I joined a group of friends for a walk on the beach. Without excusing myself, I walked towards the surf. I just needed to be alone for a few minutes. I loved feeling the water washing over my bare feet. As fate would have it, I again had a seizure and when I fell, the current started pulling me into the sea.

One of my friends realised I was drowning and just before I disappeared under a big wave, she managed to grab some of my hair and pulled me back onto the beach. Everyone went into a panic because I wasn't breathing and I had no pulse. My friend Ann stayed calm and started resuscitating me; the rest of the people were frantic. They thought I was gone. When I suddenly coughed, gasping for breath, they all just looked at each other. For years, they spoke about witnessing a miracle.

I had an epiphany: If I had indeed died the night before, what legacy would I have left for my son?

When they later put me into bed, I was completely worn-out. I woke up the next afternoon, but when I opened my eyes I remembered everything clearly: I was alone and I sat there thinking about my life and what I was doing to myself, that I was certainly on the wrong path. I had an epiphany: If I had indeed died the night before, what legacy would I have left for my son? I realised then how it was so easy for my mother to drown her problems in alcohol because I was doing the same thing! For the first time, I truly understood how easily you can become stuck in self-destruct mode. I was becoming everything that I vowed never to become. That realisation was my turning point. I knew with certainty I was given another chance. I was going to get my life back on track again.

I forced myself to focus on my surroundings and I started taking my medication regularly. I cut down on my drinking and treated the people around me with more respect. For the first time in months, I was taking care of my appearance. I was still plagued by mood swings and bouts of aggression, but I found ways to manage my feelings.

Until then, working was not a priority because we had enough money to survive on, but I knew keeping busy would be the best therapy for me. So instead of seeking out a psychologist, I talked myself into a manager position in a nearby restaurant. The restaurant was not doing well, but I managed to turn its profits around without the benefit of knowing the hospitality industry. I scoped out opposition restaurants, introduced theme parties and specials, and I jacked up the menu. I realised I still had the Midas touch, and I often wondered why I created all the chaos and insecurity.

I also realised I neglected the positive outlook that inspired me before. I wasn't living my dream and in the words of Rhett Butler in *Gone with the Wind*; I couldn't give a damn about the vow I made: "As God is my witness, I will never go hungry again!"

Once I started working, my ambition returned with full force. I had no idea what I was going to do, but I knew it was the end of my sabbatical. I said goodbye to my friends in Amanzimtoti and we headed back to Johannesburg.

The Domino Effect

 ANCHOR

> *"The cracks were already there, but now they began to split open wider and wider, and the difference between how a thing appears and the reality of what is happening suddenly becomes alarmingly clear – everything all at once, and the walls fall like dominos."*
>
> – Ronèl M Harris

This part of my story can only be described as a row of dominos standing upright and when one fell down, it took all the others with it.

My marriage had failed. My father resurfaced. My mother had taken ill. My past had once again invaded my present, and the dominos were now starting to fall, one by one.

Now we can take any one of these situations and look at them individually and they would warrant an entire chapter by themselves, but I want us to look at the overall effect this stress had on me.

My health, my relationships, my work . . . everything just fell apart, to the point where I sold everything I owned, divorced Riaan and took my son and left.

And the dominoes tumbled . . .

> *My marriage had failed. My father resurfaced. My mother had taken ill. My past had once again invaded my present, and the dominos were now starting to fall, one by one.*

COMPASS

> *"I promise you nothing is as chaotic as it seems. Nothing is worth diminishing your health. Nothing is worth poisoning yourself into stress, anxiety, and fear."*
> – Steve Maraboli, *Unapologetically You: Reflections on Life and the Human Experience*

> *I believe that the reason for becoming overwhelmed by stress is that your life is unbalanced, and this is the cause of the domino effect. The minute one falls, they all fall down.*

The effects of emotional stress for many of us have become a way of life. Stress isn't always bad. In small doses, it can help you perform under pressure and motivate you to do your best. But when you're constantly running in fight or flight mode, your mind and physical health will start paying the price. The most common cause of the domino effect is that there was no balance to begin with.

Have you ever thought about just packing a bag and leaving – "destination unknown" – because your life just seems too chaotic?

I believe that the reason for becoming overwhelmed by stress is that your life is unbalanced, and this is the cause of the domino effect. The minute one falls, they all fall down.

VOYAGE

> *"The mind can go either direction under stress – toward positive or toward negative: On or off. Think of it as a spectrum whose extremes are unconsciousness at the negative end and hyperconsciousness at the positive end. The way the mind will lean under stress is strongly influenced by training."*
> – Frank Herbert, *Dune*

Your ability or inability to tolerate stress depends on many factors, including the quality of your relationships, your general outlook on life, your emotional intelligence, and your family history. Mostly, it's how well you balance all of the mentioned factors in your life.

Leading a balanced life can be extremely difficult, especially when it starts to feel like everything is happening all at once – creating and maintaining rhythm and harmony in your life is no easy task, but one well worth learning. The easiest way to find balance is to start with your internal balance – the bits you are in control of: Getting enough sleep, eating a healthy balanced diet, exercising regularly and spending time on the things you like doing. Keeping your mind and your body healthy will strengthen your external balance such as work, relationships, social activities and family/extended family.

"If you stop chasing the wrong things, you give the right things a chance to catch you."

– Lolly Daskal

CHAPTER 13

Coming Home

In early 1997, I made the decision to move back to Johannesburg. I knew it was time to rebuild my life to make amends for all the wrongs I did before I left to try to salvage the relationships with the people I had hurt. I was wracked with guilt. I knew that earning their forgiveness was not going to be easy, but the only way that I could rebuild my life was if I started there. I realised that, at some point in my life, I had entered a phase of searching for happiness in all the wrong places. I had the mindset that happiness came from things or even people outside of myself, and that was wrong. Happiness can't be found in external things; happiness comes from within. If you want to be truly happy, you have to be grateful first and foremost for where you are in your own life, then by extension all the blessings in your life, especially those that come in the form of the people who supported you through some of the most difficult times of your life.

Leaving wasn't easy. My mother, who I as I mentioned before had taken with me to Natal so that I could take care of her after her last big stroke, had managed to find love! Charles (a widower of many years older than my mother) whom we met through friends was immediately taken with her. It was so funny. My mother, even in her diminished state (she couldn't talk and needed help with everything) didn't want anything to do with the "old man"! But he was persistent, finally winning her over. He took such good care of her! After they married, they stayed on in the park home I had purchased. The entire family was unhappy with me for letting her stay, but I felt that she deserved a bit of happiness. I knew that she would be fine with Charles.

Arriving in Johannesburg, I had to temporarily move into a spare room with friends Mandy and Buck (not their real names). Leon, then 11 years old, went to stay with Riaan so that he could have stability. He attended school while I found employment as well as a new home for us.

Leon was happy to be back in Johannesburg with his father and the rest of his friends and family. Our relationship started taking a turn for the better – his resentment towards me for moving and the events preceding the move was lessening, but I knew it would take time for everyone involved. I worked hard at repairing the rifts I had caused.

> *I realised that, at some point in my life, I had entered a phase of searching for happiness in all the wrong places. I had the mindset that happiness came from things or even people outside of myself, and that was wrong.*

I was still finding my feet when my friend organized a dinner party. She told me to be there for a surprise. I'll let you guess what the surprise was. John! They had also only told him that he needed to come to dinner for a surprise, but he figured it out. In his excitement to see me, he almost jumped out of his car before parking properly! We were so happy to see each other; we laughed and hugged for a long time! Even though we hadn't seen each other for two years, we immediately fell back into the comfortable joking manner that we used to have when he first became a family friend while I was still married to Riaan.

The next evening he came over, we started reminiscing about old times and sharing two years' worth of news. We laughed and talked until the early hours of the morning, completely oblivious of the time. When he told me that he had gone to Natal to look for me but couldn't find me, I was struck with emotion when I considered the magnitude of what that meant. He had driven all the way there, and spent time looking for me (he may eventually have found me as he came very close to where I was!). After everything that had happened, I started realizing then that he was different, that he truly cared about me. The sentiment behind that gesture is still a treasured memory and forms part of our beautiful relationship.

We started seeing more of each other – dinner dates, movies, coffee, just spending time together talking. It was one night during dinner with our friends that Buck suggested I give him my Curriculum Vitae for a car sales position he knew was opening up. I laughed so loud at the suggestion! I mean, I knew absolutely nothing about cars, except that I liked certain shapes or colours, never mind selling them! Well, Buck insisted and John encouraged me to apply, so I did. To my huge surprise, I was given the job. I must admit that I still smile when I think about it. I learned fast for the first few months. Soon, I was earning enough commission as a top sales person to afford a place of my own.

By this time my relationship with John had developed so close that we started discussing the pros and cons of moving in together. We both had similar ideas of what we needed, our similarities such as our shared love for nature helped. We easily found our first home. When we first moved in, we had nothing; we could not even hire a television! I had only just started earning a decent salary. Leon moved in with us. We were barely settled in when we received news that Charles had passed away. I went to Natal to collect my mother and she came to live with us. I have to say how I admired John's patience during this time; I learned so much about the type of person he is. Remember, he went from being a bachelor on his own, doing what he wanted, when he wanted, to suddenly having a house full of people.

We had been living together for almost a year when I woke up one morning, sick as a dog; I thought there was something majorly wrong so I went to the doctor. I was not prepared for his diagnosis – I was three months pregnant! I just sat there in shock. My mind immediately recalled the memories of six miscarriages and all I could think of was that I could not go through that again. The intense fear mixed with the excitement that followed the news surprised me, and I could barely process it.

John had asked me to marry him on a previous occasion but I had said no. I didn't want anything to change between us as we were so happy. I didn't want to complicate our lives; we loved each other, we were happy together, and to me that was enough. When I told him the news that I was pregnant, he was blown away, his excitement was overwhelming and he said now we have to get married to which my answer was no – again. Looking back, I think it was that 'have to' that made me say no. It was partly the fear of another miscarriage . . . what would happen to our relationship if I said yes and I lost the baby? I also still felt that maybe getting married would change everything! Leon was also completely shocked at the news that he was getting a baby brother or sister! He couldn't believe that at 33 I was going to have a new baby – typical teenager, he was worried about how it would look that a 14 year old suddenly had a baby sibling!

> *During the period shortly after our wedding, all my insecurities started resurfacing. I was at home taking care of our son and our home, and I had nothing to do. I stopped taking care of my appearance, as I was so conflicted.*

Our lives suddenly became very complicated two weeks after I found out I was pregnant. I was lifting my mother from the bath and almost miscarried! After rushing to the doctor he informed us that if I wanted to keep the baby, I would have to be on bed rest in the hospital. This meant that I wouldn't be able to work or take care of my mother anymore. Suddenly, we went from a two-income household to one. I had to find someone who could take care of my mother, as none of my siblings were able financially. Finally, we found a nursing home where she could receive the care she needed.

I started helping John with his business out of sheer boredom from doing nothing but lying in bed all day. I eventually took over the bookings for the lodge, as well as fixing the programs that they ran daily. My brainchild, Outdoor Education Africa, started taking shape during this stage.

After the birth of our son, we found and moved into a bigger house when John brought up the subject of getting married again. This time I said yes. I had given it a lot of thought, and I had come to realise that this is the stability that both boys would need – the foundation of family, a mother and father happily married.

When our son was a month old, we had a small intimate wedding in our new home. We didn't have any money to spare so I did all the preparations myself with the help of my friend Mandy who organized flowers. I made the decorations, we even had a cake, and in the end, it was it was a wonderful ceremony, which only our closest friends and family attended.

During the period shortly after our wedding, all my insecurities started resurfacing. I was at home taking care of our son and our home, and I had nothing to do. I stopped taking care of my appearance, as I was so conflicted. I loved being a mother again and taking care of our baby, but I also felt cheated that John could go out to work every day doing what he loved while I had given up my independence again. I missed being around people, learning new things. The house felt like it was closing in on me and I was lonely. Bored with the same daily routine, I became more and more frustrated and irritable.

> *Something inside me told me that this was my little girl that I had prayed so long for. I sincerely believed that God would bless me with a little daughter, a little girl who would grow up in a loving, secure home.*

Our evenings together changed dramatically. We no longer chatted for hours like we used to. Our conversations mostly consisted of small talk centred around the boys, the house and John's day. I felt like I had nothing to contribute, and as a result we spoke less and less, or everything turned into an argument. I felt like I had slipped into the housewife role again, which was definitely not what I wanted to be. I had gone through too much, grown too much to be happy just being a housewife – I took my frustrations out on John.

This added much strain on our marriage, but the one thing that kept us together was that both of us were too stubborn to admit defeat! Almost from the day we met again, when I came back to Johannesburg, we recognized that the friendship, love and respect we had for each other was extraordinary – once in a lifetime. Because we had such a close relationship, we recognised the warning signs that signalled that we were drifting apart. Waking up one morning, we spoke at length about all the feelings I was having about my role, about our marriage, where we were heading. We both felt committed to making our marriage work. We sought help and after working through the counselling together, we were stronger than ever. We made time to connect with each other to talk about everything that was bothering either of us. From then on, we have continued working on us…it was the start of us becoming the formidable team we are today. We work together and we encourage each other to achieve our goals.

Three years after our son was born, we had worked through the rough patches when we once again received a massive surprise – I was pregnant! I was terrified as the doctors had warned that getting pregnant again could seriously jeopardise my health. The exact opposite happened. My health was fine, it was an easy pregnancy. Something inside me told me that this was my little girl that I had prayed so long for. I sincerely believed that God would bless me with a little daughter, a little girl who would grow up in a loving, secure home. A little girl who would look at her father with love and respect.

We didn't know if I was expecting a boy or a girl until the day she was born, but I soon understood why God, in His infinite wisdom, had made me wait for her. The birth of our son taught me so much about myself and about John – I had faith in him as a father. Today, I believe if I had had my daughter first, I would have been overprotective. I would have denied her the close bond she now has with her father by projecting my own insecurities onto her. There was something very special between them since the day she was born; it grows stronger every day.

John took to being a father like a duck to water, first with Leon, who he loved like his own son, then with our own two children. To some extent, I suppose it was because of his own family history – he grew up in boarding schools and never had a close relationship with his parents. He loves being a father, being part of a family.

It was four months after our daughter was born that I was back to working full day with John at the Lodge. A year later, I officially went on my own, running my small youth tour company that would become Outdoor Education Africa, which today is one of the biggest youth tour operators in South Africa.

John and I work as hard on our marriage as we do in our businesses. We are constantly finding new ways to improve on our relationship. We make time for each other outside of work where we have a no 'shop-talk' rule! We also check in on each other during the day, just to say hi. The same goes for our children. Leon runs one of our companies from the same premises and at some point during the day, you will find him in either John's office or mine touching base on the progress with new clients or just checking in. The two younger ones also know that they can call either of us at any time during the day and we will stop what we are doing and talk a bit.

After all the hardship and the years of lessons I had to learn the hard way, I look at my life, my marriage and my family and I can honestly say, this is my reward for not giving up. I am fully aware that the road ahead will still have its challenges, but I am confident that I will be able to deal with them.

Is it possible for a home to be people and not a brick structure? To me that is exactly what being home means – with my family. I AM HOME.

Live And Learn

ANCHOR

> "Well, we all make mistakes, dear, so just put it behind you. We should regret our mistakes and learn from them, but never carry them forward into the future with us."
>
> – L.M. Montgomery, *Anne of Avonlea*

Deciding to come home meant admitting that I had made a mistake by running away in the first place. It meant admitting the mistakes I made in how I handled the separation and divorce from Riaan, taking Leon away from the only father he knew and the extended family.

Not only did I admit them, I was also determined to try and make amends for them.

> *You shouldn't get discouraged if at first they seem hesitant to forgive you; let your actions speak louder than your words. Show them that the remorse you feel is real and don't give up.*

What I learnt from this and what you need to remember here is that if the mistakes you made affected other people, it may take a very long time to earn their trust again, if at all. You shouldn't get discouraged if at first they seem hesitant to forgive you; let your actions speak louder than your words. Show them that the remorse you feel is real and don't give up. Unfortunately, there will be some people who may choose not to forgive and you will have to make peace with that. You can't force them. Know that you tried, forgive yourself and move on.

When you know that you have honestly done everything you possibly can to right your mistakes, stop being so hard on yourself.

COMPASS & VOYAGE

> *"We all make mistakes, have struggles, and even regret things in our past. But you are not your mistakes, you are not your struggles, and you are here NOW with the power to shape your day and your future."*
>
> – Steve Maraboli, *Unapologetically You: Reflections on Life and the Human Experience*

When you are able to look back on your path through life with an open mind and a kind heart, you will be able to see where you made your biggest mistakes and, sometimes, even what lead to them. Becoming connected with yourself will allow you to correct your actions as you go along. That being said, there are some mistakes, which, if you are able to avoid altogether, will make life a whole lot easier.

My Number 1 mistake is LOSING SIGHT OF MY DREAMS.

Now you need to remember that I am sharing my opinion with you about mistakes that I think cause the most harm and how you can avoid making them. You may have your own list and I suggest you write them down alongside ways to avoid or fix them.

My Number 1 mistake is LOSING SIGHT OF MY DREAMS. Do you remember what your dreams were before you started making a living instead of a life? What were your dreams for your life before you were swallowed up by responsibilities of being a functioning adult?

Fix It: Take a moment, grab a notepad and write down what your dreams are/were and honestly evaluate what has become of them. Evaluate where you are on your path and the things that you are doing daily. Are you still pursuing your dreams, or are you just making a living?

> *Running away solves nothing and letting fear stop you from trying something new steals away future happiness.*

Number 2 is LETTING FEAR CLOUD MY VISION. Fear should only keep you out of harm's way when the danger is real, not because of your perception or your imagination making you fearful. Fear of failure, fear of success, fear of past mistakes repeating themselves, fear of the unknown – so many unfounded fears can stop you from moving forward in your life and actively pursuing new goals. If you allow it, your fears will take over your entire existence.

Fix It: What you need to do is write down your fears divide them into two columns under real or assumed/imaginary. By doing this, you put your power back in your own hands.

Number 3 is FEELING OBLIGED TO HELP OTHERS AT MY EXPENSE. Being able and willing to help others is noble BUT not when the cost to you becomes overbearing.

Fix It: Figure out why you feel the need to help others. Is it because you feel you have to, because you owe them something? Do you give too much of yourself to feel accepted or even loved? I'm not saying don't help. What I am saying is help others to help themselves.

Number 4 is LIVING IN DENIAL or DENYING REALITY. This means not facing difficult situations or avoiding difficult conversations.

Fix It: Living in denial causes unnecessary strain, tension and inner turmoil. Facing the truth of the situation or having the difficult conversation will only cause temporary discomfort but permanent peace of mind.

I believe these are the four biggest mistakes that we can make, but should avoid making at all costs. Running away solves nothing and letting fear stop you from trying something new steals away future happiness.

What are yours?

"Once you start recognizing the truth of your story, finish the story. It happened but you're still here, you're still capable, powerful, you're not your circumstance. It happened and you made it through. You're still fully equipped with every single tool you need to fulfill your purpose."

— Steve Maraboli,
Life, the Truth, and Being Free

CHAPTER 14

Montclare *Revisited*

For years, I was driving up and down Main Road passing Montclare without giving it a second thought. It was a chapter in my life that I had closed and I don't dwell in the past.

It may have been because I was in the process of writing this book and that I had refreshed the memories in my mind that I noticed Loonat & Sons, the local shop on the corner where we used to buy on 'the book'. It dawned on me that the place still looked exactly the same from the outside.

> *I saw the lamppost where I sat and cried. I remembered the Good Samaritan, Aunty Grieta, offering me a plate of food.*

I remember how I had walked the same road to the little shop on the corner – I was reminded of the humiliation I used to feel when I had to go beg for a little more credit, so I could buy a piece bread or a packet of maize meal so that there would be something on the table to eat.

Curious to see what the rest of the old neighbourhood looked like, I turned into the road leading down to our old house.

The house looked nothing like I remembered it and if it wasn't for the street name and the number, I would have driven straight past it. I saw the lamppost where I sat and cried. I remembered the Good Samaritan, Aunty Grieta, offering me a plate of food.

Passing Richard's house, I was reminded of running down the road – away from the hurt and pain, but most of all his betrayal of my trust – but there was no emotion connected to those long ago memories.

I was happy to see the renovations they had made to the clubhouse at the sports field. So many good memories – that feeling of someone believing in me, working together to achieve a goal, the laughter, acceptance – it drove me to want to be the best I could be, not just for me but for the team, remembering the kindness that was shown to me and the memory of being chosen for the Southern Transvaal Team.

I sure had come a long way since then. I smiled when I remembered a song that I used to listen to many times over and over, and I remembered the promise I made many years ago that one day I would come back and play that song again.

My past is part of me. It made me who I am. It made me stronger.

Michael Bolton had a hit song, "When I'm Back On My Feet Again", that I primarily associated with this chapter of my life. I searched the playlist on my phone and there it was! I played it with the volume as loud as it could go as I drove away.

When I returned to my office, my personal assistant, Anni, asked me, "Are you okay?"

I told her yes, I revisited Montclare. I smiled because I saw that day just how far I had come. I felt pride in myself for everything that I had accomplished.

My past is part of me. It made me who I am. It made me stronger. It taught me that it doesn't matter where you come from – you have a choice what your future will be, and for this I am extremely grateful.

It taught me commitment and perseverance, and that no matter what your circumstances in life, if you have enough passion, you can realise your dreams – you are the creator of your destiny.

Life has put me through so many obstacles and tested me many times and, yes, I failed many times, but today I realise that by not giving up, accepting what you can't change and learning from it will make you a winner.

I never expected pity for my circumstances – although I sometimes felt sorry for myself, I have never used my past as an excuse.

I allowed myself to acknowledge my achievements in life – from where I was to where I had come.

What concerned me the most about my visit to Montclare that day, and still does, is that there are so many 'Montclares' not only in South Africa, but all over the world, and I worry about the people who live there and I can only hope that they – like me – have not given up their hopes and dreams, have not accepted the cards that life has dealt them. I am especially worried about the young people: Do they dream? Do they work towards a better life? Will they be able to spread their wings and break free?

> *God was always there. He let me fall so that I could learn - but He never let me fall out of His hands!*

It breaks my heart to think that many of the children born into unfortunate circumstances will eventually end their lives there, never knowing or experiencing another life. But there is also the hope of a few little 'Sonskyns' who will break out of that mould and stand tall, and make something of themselves.

I opened up my laptop. My screensaver is a picture of a lotus flower. To me, it holds a special symbolism of daily renewal because every night, the beautiful flower disappears into murky waters only to re-emerge when the sun rises the next morning without blemish. Its spotless beauty as it springs from the mud holds spiritual promise. It represents purity of the human body, speech and mind; of elegance, beauty and perfection; purity and grace. The unfolding of its petals signifies an explosion of the soul.

Fanciful as it may sound, I saw myself in that flower and I could finally put Montclare behind me.

I am not bitter – I am thankful. I have learnt to change what I can and to accept what I can't. You are the creator of your own destiny.

My message is a message of hope. I have fallen many times, but I realise that even though our relationship wasn't always as strong as it is now, God was always there. He let me fall so that I could learn – but He never let me fall out of His hands!

Breaking The Mould

 ANCHOR

> "Some people live in cages with bars built from their own fears and doubts. Some people live in cages with bars built from other people's fears and doubts; their parents, their friends, their brothers and sisters, their families. Some people live in cages with bars built from the choices others made for them, the circumstances other people imposed upon them. And some people break free."
> – C. JoyBell C.

All those years ago, I could have chosen to stay in Montclare instead of leaving with Aunty Rita. I could have accepted my fate. I didn't.

I cannot clearly remember a single day that I ever said to myself, "Well, Ronèl, this is it, this is who you are, this is all that you are ever going to be so you might as well accept it." But then I have always been a very stubborn person and I would most likely not have listened to myself anyway!

Just as hardship has a 'face', so does giving up, and neither one is pretty.

How many people just accept what they are given in life without ever challenging anything about their circumstances? Like the people I saw in Montclare that day – for all I know they could have been the very same people who were there, sitting on their porches and standing at their gates all those years ago.

Just as hardship has a 'face', so does giving up, and neither one is pretty.

Why is it then that only some people are able to break free from their moulds?

I believe that it has nothing to do with luck but everything to do with hard work and perseverance, and the conscious decision to never stop dreaming of a better life.

I believe that we all have the ability to make choices in life no matter what circumstances you are born into. You have the ability to choose to accept the situation or not.

This doesn't not just apply to being born into unfortunate circumstances either – when everything in life comes on a silver platter, it is just as easy to accept that and live within that mould too, taking everything you have for granted and, yes, not having any dreams or ambitions that drive you to do what you are passionate about.

Both sides of that coin are equal to a life wasted . . .

 COMPASS

> *"Your passion is your internal compass that will guide you from where you are towards where you want to go."*
> – Julie Connor, *Dreams to Action Trailblazer's Guide*

Do you ever wonder why things have to turn out the way they do?

Why does it happen that two children with the same circumstances can turn out so differently?

Have you ever used the circumstances you were born into as an excuse for where you are in your life?

How many people do you know do this: Always blaming everything and anyone else for where they are in their lives?

This chapter is as much about not accepting your fate as it is about accepting your past but choosing not to be a prisoner of it. When you were born, you didn't have a say in the family you were born into, but when you were growing up, you started learning that you did have a choice about where you would end up.

What you did with that choice is the important issue here.

 **VOYAGE**

> *"Belief driven by determination is one key factor governing whether what you pursue becomes real or not."*
> – Steven Redhead, *The Solution*

Value all experiences – good or bad, happy or sad – for the lessons they teach. But make sure you learn all those lessons well as they will serve their purpose in your life as tools to guide you. It is vital to remember that if you do not learn, especially from mistakes, you will keep repeating those mistakes over and over until you have learned the lesson.

Focus on the kind of life you do want, not on the one you were born into.

Focus on the kind of life you do want, not on the one you were born into.

Surround yourself with people who manifest those characteristics and who encourage you and drive you.

Avoid and eliminate negativity at all costs. Stop blaming circumstance.

Create and manifest the life that you deserve.

"I think the first step is to understand that forgiveness does not exonerate the perpetrator. Forgiveness liberates the victim. It's a gift you give yourself."

– T. D. Jakes

CHAPTER 15

Forgiveness

I have shared my life with you, I laid bare my most private and secret feelings. I told of my successes and also my failures.

Forgiving my mother and father was single-handedly the hardest thing I've ever had to do. Through all the trials and tribulations I battled, but this was an all-out war – a war I had to wage with myself.

So consumed was I by years of resentment, bottled rage, debilitating fear and loathing, I could not even contemplate forgiveness. I particularly resented my mother and for many years, I could not fathom her lack of responsibility and accountability. But now I am simply saddened by her wasted life. She came to a pitiable and helpless end. Fortunately, I no longer feel the anger that plagued me for so many years.

> *Forgiving my mother and father was single-handedly the hardest thing I've ever had to do.*

I think she blamed me for her husband, my father, leaving her. I believe she viewed me as another one of his mistresses she had to compete with – the most disturbing thought of all.

She suffered five strokes in her late 40s and early 50s, and although we were not close after all the years of bitterness, I made sure she was well looked after until she died. She was my mother and the years had softened me towards her. I had come to realise that she, in the only way she knew, was also just trying to overcome her own disappointments in life. I do know, however – I could feel it – that she wanted to tell me that she loved me. She could not speak anymore, but in my heart I knew that was what she wanted to tell me.

One evening after I attended to her, I was about to turn around when she made an almost frantic gesture to grab my arm, compelling me to look into her eyes. I know I did not imagine the love I saw in that look. It was the last time I saw her and when she died, I was thankful for those last precious moments; that we had made peace that I had finally felt her love for me. This is how I choose to remember her. When she died, I had already forgiven her for everything. I arranged a small funeral and we all said goodbye to her in a dignified way.

In my father's case, I remained steadfast in my apprehension and distrust of him. Although he begged for forgiveness many times, I just could not find it in myself to give it to him. How could I forgive that he stole my innocence and my childhood? I am a reasonable person; however, I don't have a problem forgiving people if they make an effort to change. But he had never given me reason to believe that he was ever going to change.

When we received a call from someone who had seen my father begging on a street corner in Witbank, we went to fetch him and, in the last years of his life, we allowed my father to stay on our farm where it was his duty to be the supervisor or caretaker in our absence. However, whenever we visited the farm with our children, they were never allowed to be alone with him, let alone sit on his lap. I know what happened to me when he picked me up to sit on his lap. He knew what my rules were. "If you dare to touch my kids, I will kill you without blinking an eye!" In the beginning, it was odd to the children that they could not spend time with grandpa, but I wouldn't budge. He and they had to accept my rules.

The last time I saw my father, we were all having a braai on the farm. He turned to me and asked if we could talk. I quietly nodded and walked away from the lapa where nobody could hear us.

"I want you to forgive me."

I just looked at him. "Let's not go there again. I have told you it is not possible." I turned away.

"Please."

"Sorry. I can't."

Without looking at him, I walked away. For the rest of the evening, I avoided his eyes.

The following Tuesday, I was driving to a client when I received a call from the little grocer near the farm, who said he hadn't seen my father since the weekend. I suddenly had a premonition that my father was not alive anymore. I phoned the farm; my inkling was validated when one of the staff said he also hadn't seen him. I called John and asked him to go the farm. When John arrived, my premonition was confirmed. I nearly crashed my car when he told me that he found my father in the cottage lying dead on the floor in a small pool of blood where he had fallen. I suspect he must have been trying to reach for his crutch. The doctor later confirmed that he had died of a heart attack.

> *We are the sum of our experiences; what happened to me in my life turned me into the person I am today and I love that person. I love who I am. I am a woman, hear me roar.*

We decided to make the farm his last resting place. No one he knew wanted to attend his burial – so in the end, it was only John and I, my youngest sister and the workers on the farm at his graveside. I was not sad, but I did question my reticence to forgive him, knowing that if I did, I would've allowed him to die in peace. For a long time thereafter, I had a recurring image of my father hovering between heaven and hell.

It was a whole year before I could go back to his grave. I stood there and just talked. I spoke to him for almost an hour, rambling on about my feelings, the anguish and the anger – about my loneliness as a young girl. I told him exactly how I felt, why it had been impossible for me to forgive him all these years.

After almost an hour, I heard myself say: "I forgive you."

Only when we can forgive ourselves will we be able to forgive others.

When I spoke those words, years of oppressive weight of hatred and anger rolled off my shoulders; the formidable burden lifted. I felt like a butterfly emerging from a cocoon.

We are the sum of our experiences; what happened to me in my life turned me into the person I am today and I love that person. I love who I am. I am a woman, hear me roar.

I have no regrets.

If only I had known the freedom of forgiveness earlier.

At last, I am worthy of my childhood nickname, Sonskyn – because I have a voice.

Forgive Because It's Good For You

 ANCHOR

> *"People have to forgive. We don't have to like them, we don't have to be friends with them, we don't have to send them hearts in text messages, but we have to forgive them, to overlook, to forget. Because if we don't, we are tying rocks to our feet, too much for our wings to carry!"*
>
> – C. JoyBell C.

One of the most difficult things I've ever had to do in my entire life was learning to forgive without ever getting an apology.

I took me a long time to realise that my hatred and refusal to forgive people in my past was holding me captive!

In my mind, one of the biggest requirements to forgive was that I needed some sort of 'acknowledgement of debt' or owning up by the person who wronged you. A simple sorry . . .

My father never took ownership for stealing my childhood and my innocence, which blocked my forgiveness. I thought I was punishing him by not forgiving him, but I did not realise I was only punishing myself.

It took me years to develop the emotional maturity to realise this, and the day I finally spoke the words "I forgive you", my whole life changed.

Forgiving my mother taught me the value of compassion. She became the woman she was because of circumstances. I came to terms with the fact that she simply didn't know any better and dealt with life through her own insecurities and fears.

 ## COMPASS

Let go of it! Forgive yourself for being human. Forgive yourself for your mistakes. Learn from them and then let them go!!

Only when we can forgive ourselves will we be able to forgive others.

Forgiving those who have hurt or harmed you comes second to the importance of being able to forgive yourself.

First, set yourself free and it will be easier to set your so-called enemies free. You must not allow the shackles of secret revenge and stubborn hatred to continue to bind you. Break loose and allow yourself to live the life you owe to yourself.

- Would you agree that when you forgive someone, you make the choice to give up your feelings of resentment?
- Do you agree that you also stop judging the person who caused you the hurt?
- Instead of harbouring feelings of revenge, resentment and judgment, do you show generosity, compassion and kindness?

Some of us find it difficult to grant reprieve for the damage done by others, which makes it more difficult to learn the lesson of forgiveness, which is the only way to set oneself free.

 ## VOYAGE

I would like you to take a minute to have a look at the following questions and answer them only when you've thought about them, truthfully:

- Do you feel that you can't forgive others until they apologize to you?
- Do you agree to forgive others only if they promise not to do what they did any more?
- Can you forget as well as forgive?

- Do you believe that others don't have to do anything special to deserve your forgiveness?
- Do you hold a grudge toward other people?
- How often do you feel resentful toward others for what they've done?

Forgiving those who have hurt or harmed you comes second to the importance of being able to forgive yourself. We walk around harbouring guilt and shame for the mistakes we have made, or we blame ourselves for the harm done to us by others.

> *"The truth is, unless you let go, unless you forgive yourself, unless you forgive the situation, unless you realize that the situation is over, you cannot move forward."*
> – Steve Maraboli, *Unapologetically You: Reflections on Life and the Human Experience*

"What is joy without sorrow? What is success without failure? What is a win without a loss? What is health without illness? You have to experience each if you are to appreciate the other. There is always going to be suffering. It's how you look at your suffering, how you deal with it, that will define you."

– Mark Twain

CHAPTER 16

Diamond *Years*

"**N**ever give up" – a motto I live my life by, as well as a lesson I have taught to each of my three children. Life will sometimes knock you down, but true success is measured by your ability to get back up. At times, it may take a little longer but take it from me, you will get stronger – as long as you refuse to quit.

It is easy to look at other people and think that it is unfair that their lives seem so 'easy'.

You and I are only human, which is why it is so easy when we are going through a difficult time to succumb to defeatism and self-pity to ask, "Why me?" or "Why did this have to happen?" or say, "The whole world is against me". It is easy to look at other people and think that it is unfair that their lives seem so 'easy' – I'm speaking from personal experience here because people look at the person I am today and think that exact same thing. You will only make yourself bitter by doing that because you don't know that person's story just like they don't know yours – like you didn't know mine until now . . .

My outlook on life changed the day that I accepted that everything in my life happened for a reason, and that the reason was that I was meant to share my story with women who may need to hear that there is hope and that they can make a better life for themselves. I realised that I had equipped myself with a unique set of tools through the years to overcome the adversity that I needed to share. I have learned that admitting to one's weaknesses is, in fact, a sign of strength and courage. We don't know everything and we don't have to know everything.

From when I was a little girl, I've always had a strong will to survive no matter how bad things were. I always tried to see the good in situations and people. It wasn't always easy and often I had to dig very deep, but I knew one thing for certain – if I allowed it: All the bad things would swallow me whole and I would never be able to come out again. Hard work and perseverance alone didn't bring me to where I am today. I had to learn how to cope with abuse, rejection, betrayal, grief, loss, fear and being judged. Each chapter in my life brought its own lessons and dealing with them brought a new set of skills I had to learn, but all those lessons brought me to where I am now . . . being able to tell you to never ever give up, to never lose hope and, most importantly, to not let all the bad experiences get the best of you. There is a saying that goes, "Every dark cloud has a silver lining." It's true. You just have to want to see it.

The way I live my life today tells a story not of entitlement but of immense gratitude, because I know that even after everything I have been through, I stood up and made a better life for myself.

When John and I were first married, I had a massive self-esteem problem. It was so bad that whenever anyone gave me an honest compliment, I would dismiss it and question the motive behind it, to the point that I may have come across as dismissive. Bigger than my self-esteem issue was my distrust of people. I smile whenever I remember how John gently coaxed me through that. Whenever he gave me a compliment and I dismissed it, he would tell me to look at myself in the mirror to see what he sees. I will always treasure these memories because it reminds me of the patience and love he has always pushed me forward with, and still does.

John and I have been partners in business for the better part of 15 years working together every day. There aren't many people who can say that they would be able to work with their husband or wife in the same offices every day, but that is exactly what makes our relationship and our partnership so unique. After all these years, we are still a team in everything we do and every decision we make.

Outdoor Education Africa is my heart project – it combines two of my passions: My love for children and my love for nature. There are many children whose circumstances at home are less than ideal and by giving them an opportunity to go on tour, I hope to provide them with a glimpse of the world outside, a chance to dream and see that the world is so much more than their current circumstances, maybe even restoring their faith in humanity. Where my two loves collide is my belief that our children will be the generation that effects the change needed in the world with regards to protecting our natural heritage. We must nurture, grow and teach our children to equip them to take care of our planet for future generations.

We are co-partners in a travel agency, a cross-channel marketing (social media) company and a product creation company called Info Products. We are constantly looking for new ventures to get involved in and we also believe in providing the people who we employ in our various companies with opportunities to grow and learn, and actively encourage them to expand their horizons.

The way I live my life today tells a story not of entitlement but of immense gratitude, because I know that even after everything I have been through, I stood up and made a better life for myself. I did not become a victim of circumstance; I did not just accept my fate. I was blessed to learn about the caring nature of strangers when we lived in Montclare. I was blessed to have had the love and support of my godparents. I was blessed to have known my first husband Leon, who showed me what romantic love in its purest form looked like when all I had was the cruel example set by my father. I was blessed to have learned family values from my second husband Riaan. By caring for my mother, and to an extent my father, I learned that my compassion was one of my greatest attributes. My biggest blessing and most treasured accomplishment is having my own family, being a mother to my children and wife to my husband, John, which I dreamed of ever since I was a little girl.

Never in my wildest dreams did I imagine that my path would lead here and that I could help others by sharing my story until John and I attended a seminar given by Bo Eason in San Diego in 2012. The moment he stepped onto the stage and started sharing his life story, I was struck with the inspiration that I too could inspire women to make the changes in their lives, which would empower them to start living the lives they could only dream about.

I have a story to tell. And I have to share my message of hope – my message about the dream that must never die.

> *I believe every person has a story to tell.*

This journey would not have been possible without the love we have for, and faith we have in, each other. We constantly push each other to do better and John's committed love has become the blueprint for the way I love people, the way I care for my family, my friends, and even the compassion I feel for people I have just met.

That same compassion is my driving force to share my story with you, whom I've never met.

When I started this book, I was terrified – sharing my story, exposing my soul to an audience meant opening myself up to being judged and, of course, my fear of being rejected. Sharing parts of my life experience that I feel could benefit others scared me, because I can't see you and your reaction while you read through these pages! I realised that the reason for sharing my story was bigger than any of my fears. I had to let other women know that it is never too late to start living the life of your dreams! The life you deserve! I had to let people know about the freedom that comes from making peace with your past and the knowledge that your past does not define you. Where you come from doesn't matter – it's where you are going that does!

Even though my next challenge is a scary one for me, I will overcome my fear so that I can teach others the same tools as I have given you in this book by sharing my story from a stage, armed only with knowledge, experience and a microphone!

I believe every person has a story to tell. It is time to take the next step in order to realise your own dreams.

Stop looking at the obstacles, stop questioning your abilities. You have read this book up to this chapter for a reason!

What is stopping you? Why are you procrastinating? Are you hesitant because of fears created by failures in your past, which caused negative perceptions, insecurities, self-doubt and a lack of confidence?

If I can help people become more self-assured and stop questioning themselves, I will be fulfilled. If just a handful of people take control of their lives by realizing that they are more than their past, more than the life they were dealt with, I would have fulfilled my dream.

Your future hinges on your dreams. The dreams in your eyes will fix your focus on the future.

When I run out of dreams, I will know it's time to stop, but in the meantime, I thank the heavens that I can share my message of hope – my message of faith.

You are the creator of your own destiny.

A Life Devoted To Gratitude

 ANCHOR

> *"It's easy to thank God and to be happy when you live a sheltered life and have no concept of suffering; suffer and then do all of the above."*
> – Donna Lynn Hope

I could have just accepted the cards life dealt me and become a bitter, beaten person. I may even have had people in my life that felt sorry for poor, sad Ronèl, saying, "Shame after everything the poor girl went through in her life, the least we can do is care for the poor miserable mess!" Sorrowful existence – it easily could have been my choice. Instead, the fighter in me chose a different approach, I challenged every card I was dealt and I not only accepted all these challenges, I tackled them head on. There were times, let's be honest, when I questioned the fairness of it all, and each time I was reminded that nobody said the game would be fair nor did it have to be. It was up to me, and how I chose to play the game.

> *There were times, let's be honest, when I questioned the fairness of it all, and each time I was reminded that nobody said the game would be fair nor did it have to be.*

I chose to call this anchor "A Life Devoted To Gratitude" because *I believe that only when you are grateful for your struggle, you are truly able to appreciate each and every blessing in your life.*

Today I can say that I am grateful, because every struggle was another lesson in how to succeed in life. It taught me survival, and now I can share my experiences to help other people.

Survival means the ability to not give up, as well as endurance and hard work.

I don't think I ever imagined how hard I would have to work to fulfil the Scarlett promise to myself that "I will never go hungry again." I still work hard – every day of my life. One can't ever take success or stability for granted.

# COMPASS

> *"Cultivate the habit of being grateful for every good thing that comes to you, and to give thanks continuously. And because all things have contributed to your advancement, you should include all things in your gratitude."*
> – Ralph Waldo Emerson

What are *you* most grateful for in *your own* life?

Can *you* single out some of the very best things in *your* life?

Perhaps you feel like me, that it is not just a case of pointing out the best things in my life or listing them in a specific order. Every blessing had its own significance. It's almost like asking a parent which of their children they love more! I love my children differently because they are unique and each one deserves to be loved in their own way. This is the way I feel about everything in my life!

There is one person I am most thankful to for encouraging me to become the person I am today. I am grateful for *his* endurance, the man who made all my dreams come true: John. Yes, our relationship wasn't always smooth sailing. We experienced stormy seas, but started working together, alongside each other not only to save our dreams, but to turn our marriage into a magical reality.

John taught me to believe in myself and our relationship is the foundation upon which we have built our lives. Again, it was, and still is, hard work. Through his respect, I learned to respect myself and accept life's blessings. Our relationship, I know, will be the yardstick our children will use to measure their partnerships.

I am grateful every day of my life to be blessed with such a wonderful compatriot, husband and friend.

VOYAGE

> *"If we never experience the chill of a dark winter, it is very unlikely that we will ever cherish the warmth of a bright summer's day. Nothing stimulates our appetite for the simple joys of life more than the starvation caused by sadness or desperation. In order to complete our amazing life journey successfully, it is vital that we turn each and every dark tear into a pearl of wisdom, and find the blessing in every curse."*
>
> – Anthon St. Maarten, *Divine Living: The Essential Guide To Your True Destiny*

I can honestly say that I am grateful for my past because . . .

- I believe that it is because I have known first-hand what it is to have nothing that **I am able to give**.
- I believe that it is because I accepted help when I needed it that **I am able to help others**.
- I believe that I can teach others to forgive because **I know what that freedom from being held captive by the inability to forgive feels like**.
- I believe that I can encourage hope because **I have known hopelessness**.

- I believe that the compassion I have for people comes from learning to understand that not everybody has the ability to cope with the storms of life. **I have learned understanding**.

What are you grateful for?

Are you able to say that you are grateful for the obstacles that brought you to where you are in your life?

> "Be grateful for obstacles across your path. They will become reminders that what you have, was worth fighting for. By choosing to be grateful and to feel blessed, you make the choice to be a happy human being."
> – Ronèl M Harris

"The will of God will never take me where the grace of God will not protect me."

– Oriah Mountain Dreamer,
The Invitation

CHAPTER 17

Full Circle

In this chapter, I first and foremost want to thank you from my heart for reading my book and for sharing this part of my journey with me. I hope that I have touched your life in some way and I would love to hear from you. I would also like to extend an invitation for you to join me on the next part of my journey by attending one of my seminars that form part of **The Diamond Personal Power Program**, where I go into even more depth teaching the tools I believe every woman needs to have to claim the life of her dreams.

So much has happened in my life while I have been writing this book: The death of my beloved godmother Aunty Rita after losing her battle with cancer, and my own personal health scare – tumours were growing on my thyroid gland and it had to be removed. I have had to completely change my diet to compensate and control my cholesterol as well. I can honestly say I feel like I have been tested these last couple of months.

> *I believe that only when you are grateful for your struggle are you truly able to appreciate each and every blessing in your life.*

Another massive turning point happened within my company. As I've told you, I have been running Outdoor Education Africa for the past 15 years armed only with my field-guides and my personal assistant. Early this year, my personal assistant resigned after being offered a position that offered her more growth than I could at that stage. I was sad to see her go, but I would never stand in anyone's way if they want to grow. This event lead me to think that maybe it was time for the company to grow and, as scary as this was, I took the step out of my comfort zone and grew my 'baby' to a 'teenager' almost overnight. I found three new team players to handle my marketing, bookings and finance departments, and I am more than pleased with the progress so far! I am amazed at how easy this change turned out to be. I know that this surprises people close to me as well, because of how protective I have always been of my company. I am looking forward to seeing their input and the fruits that will come from this growth spurt.

This chapter is mainly about gratitude because I believe that *only when you are grateful for your struggle are you truly able to appreciate each and every blessing in your life.*

> *The decisions we make in our lives should benefit others as well as ourselves; when decisions are made using the wisdom of lessons learnt, you will be making empowered, fearless decisions.*

I am grateful for the blessing of my marriage and my family. To be able to provide the safety and security that I never had as a child to my children means the world to me. I cannot even begin to describe the warm feeling I get from my adoring children when they wake up in the morning. John is my rock and a wonderful father to our children. He sets such a wonderful example of how to be steadfast in pursuit of your goals and what it means to live your values. I really couldn't have asked for a better man to restore my views on what being a family unit means. As a family, we do everything together, from planning outings to solving problems and setting goals for us as a family.

The one very important thing I learned that I must share with you is that a beautiful marriage or relationship takes hard work and effort from both sides – much like planting a garden, you have to plant the seeds and water it, nurture it, keep it safe in order for it to grow and become beautiful. It won't always be easy to keep the sparkle and the romance alive, but when you both want to you can stay as in love with each other as when you first started dating, you will make the effort.

I am grateful for the handful of people that I call my close friends. They know everything about me and love me regardless; they have allowed me in their lives, and the mutual love and respect we share is absolutely priceless. I have so many precious memories from shared adventures, ups and downs, happiness and sadness over the years, which I would not change for anything. Because of them, I have learned that there are wonderful people in this world, and the snide remarks from people in my past are drowned out by genuine conversations. Those memories no longer make me doubt others or myself.

John and I place the same importance on values such as respect and honesty in our relationship. Through the years, I have learned not to make assumptions or to jump to conclusions, which I believe are two of the biggest causes of disunity in a relationship. We make time for each other to talk about where we are, where we are going and what we want to achieve in our marriage and our lives.

If I had to choose one value, I would say that honesty is on top of my list. Being honest to people is the true measure of who I am as a person and because I live it, and I expect it from everyone I associate with. I do not tolerate falseness or lies in any way, shape or form. I believe we should all live our lives with integrity.

Right below honesty on my list I will put trust – it used to be hard for me to trust people and accept support from them without thinking they are out to get me or they want something from me. I am grateful that the people in my life have taught me that this is not always the case. I am grateful that I can earn the trust of others as well, and that I am able to offer support when there is a need, without feeling like they are using me or taking advantage of me.

I didn't have any physical role models growing up; however, I have people I look up to now, such as Sir Richard Branson, who, even though he also came from humble beginnings, has made a success of his life and strives to empower the people he takes along on his journey through life. He lives a humble life and constantly gives back through his charity work and is an active campaigner for the ethical treatment of people in the workforce. Another person I admire for his contribution to the well-being of others is Tony Robbins. His ability to change people's lives as well as his organization that raises donations for food for the needy is nothing short of admirable.

What I feel I have in common with them is a survival instinct, which to me means the ability to not give up, to have endurance and to work hard, to fight for what you believe in.

When we can understand that we are all individually responsible for the paths we choose to take in life, for our mistakes and accepting that sometimes we make the wrong decisions, owning up to them and learning from them, then we will truly be free from blame and guilt and the shackles of our past. I try hard to make better decisions that are unselfish and properly thought through, but I still make mistakes. However, I am a lot less hard on myself. The decisions we make in our lives should benefit others as well as ourselves; when decisions are made using the wisdom of lessons learnt, you will be making empowered, fearless decisions. I chose to rise above the circumstances of my past. I chose to rise above the abuse and break the cycle, and refused to give in to the victim mentality. I chose to dream of a better life and to this day, I have not stopped dreaming. I chose to forgive to set myself free.

Over the past years, my faith has become a very powerful part of my life. I realise that not only does God have a purpose for us all, there is a reason for every single thing that happens in our lives as well. Life becomes easier when we stop questioning why things happen and rather ask what it is that God would like us to achieve or learn from the experience. When we stop trying so hard to do everything by ourselves and let God show us the way, life becomes so much easier. I thank God every day for the blessings in my life and I know that without allowing Him to lead my decisions, they may not turn out right. I have come a long way in my relationship with God, which started out with my father's warped example of what he thought religion was. I'm not preaching or trying to convert you. I believe religion is a very personal choice we make and whether you are religious or not, that choice remains yours alone.

It is difficult to imagine the violence and chaos that marked the early years of my life when I am with my own family sharing jokes and laughter around the dinner table at the end of every day. Or to associate with the clumsy welfare housing estate in Montclare when I look at the beautiful sunset from a vantage point on our farm, where, just before dusk, we can see Rhett and Scarlett as they turn, before gracefully strolling off into the night. To me, they have to be the most beautiful giraffes in the whole of Africa.

I have come full circle, but I am far from finished . . .

Your Destiny, Your Story

 ANCHOR

> *"The best teachers have showed me that things have to be done bit by bit. Nothing that means anything happens quickly – we only think it does. The motion of drawing back a bow and sending an arrow straight into a target takes only a split second, but it is a skill many years in the making. So it is with a life, anyone's life. I may list things that might be described as my accomplishments in these few pages, but they are only shadows of the larger truth, fragments separated from the whole cycle of becoming."*
>
> – Joseph Bruchac, author, playwright, musician

Are the ghosts of your past holding you hostage or are you simply too scared to disrupt the status quo?

Just like me, you are also still living your story. Think about the person you are today: How did you get to be this person? What are your hopes and dreams, your fears and doubts? Look at the people in your life – pretend for a moment that you are the director of the movie of your life and they are the actors, and they each have a role that they play. Are you happy that they are the best people for the part? Then look at yourself as the main character – are you?

Are you living the life of your dreams, the life you were destined for?

COMPASS

> *"There are winds of destiny that blow when we least expect them. Sometimes they gust with the fury of a hurricane; sometimes they barely fan one's cheek. But the winds cannot be denied, bringing as they often do a future that is impossible to ignore."*
>
> – Nicholas Sparks, *Message in a Bottle*

If you are finding yourself hesitant to make changes in your life, I would like to urge you to take a long hard look at what is making you feel like that. Are the ghosts of your past holding you hostage or are you simply too scared to disrupt the status quo?

I want to tell you (like I once needed to be told) that you are an amazing human being! You are capable of living a wonderful fulfilled life – the life of your dreams! You just have to want it bad enough!

 **VOYAGE**

> *"What we call our destiny is truly our character and that character can be altered. The knowledge that we are responsible for our actions and attitudes does not need to be discouraging, because it also means that we are free to change this destiny. One is not in bondage to the past, which has shaped our feelings, to race, inheritance, background. All this can be altered if we have the courage to examine how it formed us. We can alter the chemistry provided we have the courage to dissect the elements."*
>
> – Anaïs Nin, *The Diary of Anaïs Nin, Vol. 1: 1931-1934*

I chose to dream of a better life and to this day, I have not stopped. DREAM!

I want to leave you with this – YOUR ATTITUDE TOWARDS YOUR LIFE, YOUR DREAMS AND YOUR DESTINY – is what will ultimately set you on the course to achieving it . . . or not.

Don't like the direction your life is going in? CHANGE IT!

You are at the helm of your ship through life; you are the captain. This life and where you want it to go is yours to choose. No one else can do it for you.

I chose to rise above my circumstances – so can you!

I chose to rise above the abuse and broke the cycle, and to refuse to give in to the victim mentality – choose it for yourself!

I chose to dream of a better life and to this day, I have not stopped. DREAM!

I chose to forgive to set myself free – you can too!

You are standing on thes threshold of a brand new beginning for the rest of your life. You stand in this moment at a beautiful new beginning, full of promise and possibility. See it, know it, live it, and allow the joy to flow more abundantly than ever before.

Make the choice to actively start chasing your destiny – now!

Scan this QR code or visit
www.facebook.com/breakfreebook
for FREE empowerment strategies that are
an extension of the book's Anchor Sections.

Scan this QR code or visit
www.tinyurl.com/DiamondPower-FB
to access The Diamond Personal Power Program
for FREE self-development tools that will
enable women to reach their fullest potential.

ARE YOU A PERSON WITH A PASSION TO TURN AN IDEA INTO A BUSINESS?

The next great entrepreneur is out there.

WILL IT BE YOU?

EXPONENTIAL ENTREPRENEURS ACADEMY

CREATING OPPORTUNITIES

- INDIVIDUAL GROWTH
- EXPONENTIAL GROWTH
- INFO TECHNOLOGY
- ONLINE BUSINESS
- ONLINE MARKETING
- VIDEO MARKETING
- ONSTAGE PRESENTATIONS
- ONLINE PUBLISHING
- PRODUCT CREATION
- 3D PRINTING

 info@infoproducts.co.za

 +2711 025 4621

 www.exponentialentrepreneursacademy.com

7 CR Swart Ave
Wilrogate, Roodepoort
Johannesburg
South Africa
1731

Ronèl M Harris

AUTHOR
ronel@ronelharris.com
+27 0 117685934
www.ronelharris.com

OTHER BOOKS RECOMMENDED BY BLACK CARD BOOKS

The Millionaire Mindset
How Ordinary People Can
Create Extraordinary Income
Gerry Robert

The Financial Toolbox
Your Best Business Guide To:
Less Tax, Greater Profit
And More Time!
Jessie Christo

Messy Manager
Double Your Sales
And Triple Your Profits
Jean-Guy Francoeur

The Happiness Effect
Business Without
The Headache
Shaun Bicego

**Powerful Habits
To Grow Younger
Every Day!**
Look And Feel 10
Years Younger —
Naturally
Wendy Vineyard

The Dream Retirement
How to Secure Your Money
and Retire Happy
Charlie Reading

Climbing Big Ben
How To Survive, Thrive
And Succeed In London
Harry Sardinas

**Obesity: It's Not A
Character Flaw**
Weight Loss Surgery
The Alternative When You're
Done With Diets (And Blame)
David E. Hargroder, M.D.

www.blackcardbooks.com

OTHER BOOKS RECOMMENDED BY BLACK CARD BOOKS

Scale Up IT
The Roadmap To Bring Your Enterprise To The Next Level
Jorge De Andrade

Living On Purpose
The Key To Change Your Life And Impact Others
Petra Laranjo

The Business Tango
Embracing Enterpreneurship & Intrapreneurship
Anna Shilina

How To Join The Mile-High Club
Your Ticket To Unlimited Potential
Des and Belinda Werner

The Ace Model
Winning Formula For Audit Committees
Sindi Zilwa

Life Sucks!
Everything You Need To Know About Living A Happy Life
Franky Ronaldy & Meow Ling Ng

Success Leaves A Trail
Fast-Track Your Success In 3 Simple Steps
David Bunney

From The Bedroom To The Boardroom
How Women Can Be Powerful & Win Big - Anywhere!
Princess Tsakani Nkambule

www.blackcardbooks.com

OTHER BOOKS RECOMMENDED BY BLACK CARD BOOKS

Enjoy Your Life Now!
How To Become Happy And Successful With Powerful Techniques
Rudi Zimmerer

Letting Purpose & Passion Drive Your Marriage
How To Find Harmony & Happiness No Matter What!
Bonnie and Dr. Jay Crandall

The Bergen Protocol
How To Achieve Your Goals
Kevin Bergen

Travel Learn Earn
Let The World Be Your Guide To Freedom!
Dr. Matthew Horkey

Unlimited Income Now
Your Fastest Path To The Biggest Cash
Dr Iqbal K M

The Reading Comprehension Guru
15 Surefire Strategies To Get Your Child To The Top Of The Class
Dr. Nora Anniesha

Secrets Of The Financially Free
How Ordinary People Achieve Extraordinary Financial Success
Sharon Woo

The Secret Code Is It For Real?
Unleash The Power Within! Boost Up Your Levels To Get Ahead In The Game Of Life!
Anm Pek

www.blackcardbooks.com

www.ingramcontent.com/pod-product-compliance
Lightning Source LLC
Chambersburg PA
CBHW050144170426
43197CB00011B/1953